BABYSITTING FOR GOD

Inspiring stories
of amazing foster children
and their incredible journeys.

Dr. Heidi McLain

*The names of these children,
and portions of their stories have been
changed for their protection.*

Babysitting For God
Inspiring stories of amazing foster children
and their incredible journeys.
by Dr. Heidi McLain

Printed in the United States of America

ISBN 978-1-60647-636-9

Questions about becoming a Foster Parent?
For information contact the National Foster Parent Association.
Phone: 800-557-5238
Email: info@NFPAonline.org
Web address: http://www.nfpainc.org/

Thank you ahead of time for supporting either of the 501(c)(3) non-profit resource centers listed below. They both serve foster children and the families who care for them. Your tax-deductible online donations, purchases from the resale store, or volunteering to help the dedicated and passionate staff, carry out the mission of meeting the physical, emotional, educational, and spiritual needs of abused and neglected children.

Straight From the Heart
Phone: 760-744-2240 FAX: 760-744-3209
Email: sftheart@sbcglobal.net
Web Address: http://www.straightfromtheheartinc.com/
(Tax ID#: 33-0883050)

Connected Through Kids
Phone: 760-743-7781 FAX: 760-743-7781
Email: information@connectedthroughkids.com
Web Address: http://www.connectedthroughkids.com/
(Tax ID#: 57-1237802)

For definitions of child abuse or reporting numbers in your area, call the Childhelp® National Child Abuse Hotline at 1-800-4-A-CHILD® (1-800-422-4453). Degreed professionals staff the hotline 24 hours a day, accepting calls from the United States, Canada, Guam, Puerto Rico and the U.S. Virgin Islands. Calls are anonymous and toll-free. State-of-the-art technology provides translators in 140 languages.

Babysitting for God
P.O. Box 28022
San Diego, CA 92198-0022
BabysittingForGod.com

www.xulonpress.com

With love and appreciation, this book is dedicated to the children who have been neglected, drug-exposed, psychologically, sexually, emotionally and physically abused, and who, *through no fault of their own* have had their lives turned upside-down; the foster parents who are in it for the *right* reasons, the social workers and their supervisors who pay attention, listen and care; the birth parents who dare to know; the relative caregivers who are taken for granted, and the non-relative caregivers who step up to the plate. It is dedicated to the adoptive parents who want to better understand their children; the teachers who know who these kids are, and want to make a *bigger* difference in their lives; the politicians and lawmakers who will *not* turn their back, but intend to make an effort to understand the brokenness of the system and *do something* to make it better; the many people who did *not* have a positive experience while in foster care; and to every person who has a heart for these children, their situation and needs, their journey and aloneness, and who are interested in making a difference so that the children might have the opportunity to grow and become all that God has created them to be. I am optimistic that this book will bring awareness to what is really going on - right here in America.

These are *our* children. The ones that *weren't*
aborted, the one's that *didn't die* from the abuse, the
fatherless! They haven't committed suicide, ended
up in a mental institution, or gone to jail, *yet.* They
need us, *now.*

"May you be blessed by the Lord,
the Maker of heaven and earth."
Psalm 115:15

CONTENTS

ACKNOWLEDGMENTS

Although *Babysitting for God* did not take long to write, and few knew it was in the works, I want to thank the many people who unknowingly made contributions that made it possible.

Thanks to my three children, Amanda, Christopher, and Bradley, who have always cheered me on in my endeavors to serve, and for my adopted daughter Anna. I am honored beyond words that, to the four of you, I am your Mom.

To my fellow foster parents whose encouragement and support meetings at all times of the day and night kept me 'in the boat.'

To my close friends who have so generously shared their lives, their love, their encouragement, and their appreciation and acknowledgment for what I do.

Jackie Stewart, whose emotional and spiritual support made the writing of this book possible.

Dr. Larry Allen, who I secretly wish every foster child could have as their father, who is and will always be one of my closest and dearest friends, and who has always been one of my biggest cheerleaders and encouragers.

My greatest debt goes to my youngest son, Bradley, for his genuine love, his loyalty, and his constant support. He has sacrificed so much for foster children. He has given up alone time with me, time with just our core family, and family vacations. Over the years, he has had to share celebrations, large and small, such as his birthday, Valentine's day, Easter, Halloween, Thanksgiving and Christmas with 3 or 4 or 5 or even 6 other children, many of whom were virtual strangers to him. It was never just me that attended back to school nights, performances, promotions, high school orientation, graduations or other school events. He missed out on some of my attention, and shared me with 300+ children over the years. My deepest prayer is that one day, any resentment that he might have for this sacrifice would dissipate and be filled with a feeling of joy, that he was part of something so incredible, and that the Lord will bless him many times over, in ways that he could never imagine. I thank you again, Bradley, for giving so sweetly your love and support. I love you.

"Give generously to Him and do so
without a grudging heart;
then because of this, the Lord your God
will bless you in *all* your work
and in *everything* you put your hand to."
Deuteronomy 15:10

GRATITUDE

Iwouldn't be me, if I didn't thank some other people that truly made a difference in my life and the lives of my foster children. Those special people include: Dr. Rosalie Easton, Lisa Ciccarelli, Dr. Skip Himelstein, Wendy and Steve Jones, Pastor Scott Gehrman, Dr. Lisa White and Bryan Truel, Greg and Danuta Kiernan, Dr. Cahleen Shrier & Covina Assembly of God, Jaci Lorrain & Family, Jane Diersing, Dr. Christy Walter, Patty Boles, Nadiene Sahagun, and Mirtha Valadez at Straight From the Heart; Nina Morgan, Dolores Keeling, Barbie Caldwell & Connected Through Kids, Dr. Sally Nelson, Dr. Joachim Schwartz, Mari Rodriquez, Dawn Rosencrance, "Suebee" Brown, Ginger deVilla-Rose, Marilyn Sproat, Brittany Rose Crayton, Pastor Dennis & Emmanuel Faith Community Church, Jamie Layne, Michael Brooks, Kelli Fiore, Donna Lawrence, Kaela von Laue, Lorrie York, Lyn and Jon Burnes, Mona and Bob Lewis, Pam White, Shana McGie, Sonia Castillo, Kimber Reed, Ann Fox, Tim Pfeiler and Escondido Mayor Lori Holt-Pfeiler, Kathleen Stark & Family, John Stearns and Lee Drury, Lucinda Lawton & 'Self Mastery' seminar, The ladies in the PTSD Group, Louie and Brooke at SurfCamps USA, Jennifer Sovay, Mark Shelton & Toyota of Escondido, John Van Doorn at North County Times, Barbara De Angelis & 'Making Love Work' seminar, Christy Carlson & G.I.F.T.S. of Giving, Dr. Laura

& *My Stuff Bag,* Dr.'s Marquez and Zarate, Anna and Elena at Escondido Family Medicine, Dr. Stanley Schaeffer & staff, Samantha Anderson, Tammy Hunter, Kathy Hovland & Sector 9, Katie Horstman and Dawn Anders & Blankets of Love, Life and Faith; Brian Szymchack & Applebee's of Escondido, Rod Bates, Laura Gates, Principal Susan Banning & the staff at LR Green Elementary School, Principal Julie Rich & the staff at Bear Valley Middle School, Laura Reyes & McKinney-Vento Program, Pamela Waleck, Paul Swiller, Carl and Mary Fielstra & Green Oak Ranch, the staff at North County Assessment Center, Klea Galasso & the staff at New Alternatives Family Visitation Center, Susie Purvis & Voices for Children, Michelle Lustig & tutors through the San Diego County Office of Education, Foster Youth Services Program and CSUSM; the many foster children that have been a part of our family and whom I will *never* forget, my ghost writer, the *Holy* Ghost, and most importantly God - who gently guided me to the center of His will for my life, and who time and time again answered my desperate prayers for a multitude of children.

"In everything I did, I showed you that by this kind
of hard work we must help the weak,
remembering the words the Lord Jesus himself said:
'It is more blessed to give than to receive.'"
Acts 20:35

INTRODUCTION

There are many aspects of foster care that can be written about - the "broken system," the stigma placed on foster parents (which is sometimes validated), the actions of parents who got their kids taken away, and even the legal drama that occurs; but the most fascinating, devastating, gratifying and poignant aspect, is the stories of the children and who they effect that can only come from within the foster family. *Babysitting For God* is both a heart-warming and heartbreaking book, with an inside look at what goes on in a loving foster home. America's children in foster care and the people who affect their lives deserve the attention and awareness this first-of-its-kind book brings. It gives a true-to-life perspective of the incredible, difficult, and sometimes unbelievable journey these innocent children encounter as they enter in, move through, and leave the foster care system.

"This will be written for the generation to come,
that a people yet to be created may praise the Lord."
Psalm 102:18 (NKJV)

STORIES

AMBER

It was late March, when I got this cute little long, brown-haired Kindergartener. Amber was only 5-years-old, and had a good attitude about most everything. She ate whatever I put in front of her, went to bed when asked to, woke right up in the morning to get ready for school, and held very still when her hair was being done. She especially loved to have it braided, and would nearly always smile and say, "Wow! Thanks! I am going to look *nice* today, aren't I!" Amber had been severely neglected by her drug-addicted mom. When I asked the social worker which school she went to, she said that the birth mom had only taken Amber to school for the first month, then stopped taking her, so for the past five months, she hadn't been to school at all. Because Amber mentioned how much she liked her teacher and missed her, and to get an idea of how she did during that month, I called the school and spoke to the teacher. She was extremely nice and recalled very quickly that Amber was at grade level for everything but her writing skills. I told her how Amber talked very fondly of her. When Amber's teacher said that a permission slip, due the next day, had not yet been returned, I asked, "What do you mean? I heard Amber only went to school for one month, back in September?" " Oh, no!" the teacher said,

15

"She's been coming every day - Sometimes a half an hour early, or a half an hour late, but she is *always* here. In fact, I don't think she has *ever* missed a day!" I was astonished! It turned out that Amber was getting herself up and ready, letting herself out of the house, walking herself to school and back, and sneaking back into her house, all without her birth mom knowing it! Dear God, thank you for your protection over Amber. Thank you for giving her the amazing determination to succeed. Lord, I pray I will always be grateful for your provisions, including all the teachers that make a difference in children's lives. Lord, please bring encouragement to all the teachers today. In Jesus' name, Amen.

> "I can do all things through Christ
> who strengthens me."
> **Phil 4:13** (NKJV)

JACK

Jack was a cute little 2-year-old boy with wispy light brown hair and green eyes. He was in foster care as the result of neglect, and thrived on all the attention he received from us. Because when we got him, he knew only five words - "Mama," "Da-da," "bye-bye," "hot," and "Coke," we excitedly made a goal to teach Jack as much as we could. We worked with him constantly, pointing out everything possible for him to repeat. He was like a little sponge. As his vocabulary increased, he went from rarely saying a word to talking quite a bit. One morning, I was leaving the school after meeting with a teacher. I put Jack in his car seat and he promptly said, "Butt hole." I gasped! Oh my gosh!!!! I couldn't *believe* it! I wondered who would teach him such a thing. When my kids got out of school that day, we had a family meeting. After all three denied teaching him that word, I responded, "Well, I suppose it doesn't *really* matter who taught Jack that. What matters is what we do from here

on out. We are *all* accountable for everything we teach him!"
Unfortunately, a few weeks went by, and Jack was *still* saying,
"butt hole." At one point, I noticed he seemed to say it much
more when we were in the car. Actually, he *only* said it when
we were in the car. Just out of curiosity, one of the older
kids asked Jack, "*Where* is the butt hole?" He smiled and
pointed to the car seat's "buck-le." All of us, including Jack,
laughed so hard. Week after week, we continued to teach
him as many new words as we could. When tested months
later, Jack was found to no longer have any developmental
delays in speech or language. The dedication and concerted
efforts of the entire family to help Jack learn, paid off.

"Vision is not enough;
it must be combined with venture.
It is not enough to stare up the steps;
we must step up the stairs."
Vaclav Havel

MACKENZIE

When 11-year-old Mackenzie came to live with us, she
was so scared she barely spoke. She had blonde hair, blue
eyes with dark eyelashes, and a very innocent look to her.
It was hard to figure out how anyone could have physically
abused her so badly. A few days after moving in with us, she
overheard me talking on the phone to a social worker about
volunteering to speak at the New Foster Parent Orientation.
After hanging up, I could tell Mackenzie was very interested to know more, and sure enough, she asked. "Mostly
it is about answering questions that a group of grown-up's
ask, that are trying to decide whether to be foster parents." I
said. "What do they ask you?" she said, talking very quietly.
"How do you *not* get attached?" and "Doesn't it hurt too
much when the child leaves?" I answered. "Then what do
you say?" she continued. "If it doesn't hurt when they leave,

you probably *shouldn't* be doing it!" I explained. Like many potential foster parents, Mackenzie wanted to know *why*. The reasoning is that it really needs to be about the *child*, and *not* about how the foster parent feels. It is best to focus on what we as a family are able to give to *them*, and even all the joy they bring to us. Perhaps the most precious gift we have to give is our love. After all, they are the ones that have had their whole world turned upside-down. Abraham Lincoln said, "To ease another's heartache is to forget one's own."

> "I give you a new commandment:
> that you should love one another.
> Just as I have loved you,
> so you too should love one another."
> **John 13:34** (AMP)

MARCUS & DARRELL

Although the situation *itself* wasn't exactly ideal, it made me happy to have Marcus and Darrell come to our home. Their mom, for the 6th time, went back to jail following a drug bust, and these little 5 and 6-year-old boys were back in the system. They were so cute and surprisingly happy to be with us. Exactly the same height and very similar facial features, they looked like twins; and in fact, we were asked many times if they were. They loved sliding down the stairs on their backsides and performing daring side flips on the trampoline. On the second afternoon with us, after talking with them about "comfort foods," I asked them what foods were on *their* list of favorites. I told them I wanted to make something for dinner that they would really like. They answered rather quickly, taking turns back and forth and without any hesitation, "Fried chicken! Greens! Sweet potatoes! Bread pudding! Baked beans! Mashed pota- toes! Ribs! White gravy!" *White gravy? What was that?* I wondered. Admittedly overwhelmed, I hadn't *ever* prepared fried chicken, and to tell the truth, I wasn't even sure what "greens" actually were. "Hmmm," I said to the boys, "While I figure out how to make some of these things, do you think McDonald's would be okay for tonight?" Marcus and Darrell screamed and jumped up and down yelling, "*Yay!!* Can we have Happy Meals??" A sigh of relief came over me. Like Mother Theresa once said, "I know God will not give me anything I can't handle. I just wish that He didn't trust me so much." It was exciting and kind of fun learning to prepare some new dishes, and my heart was definitely in the right place, but once Marcus and Darrell took the first few bites of my food, they almost simultaneously, with cute smiles on their faces said, "This food is *nasty*, Miss Heidi!" As I had many, many times in the past, I couldn't help but wish we had more African American foster parents on board.

"Everybody can be great...
because anybody can serve."
"You don't have to have a college degree to serve.
You don't have to make your subject and verb agree
to serve. You only need a heart full of grace.
A soul generated by love."
Dr. Martin Luther King, Jr.

EMMA

Sometimes, as a foster parent, you don't completely realize how great the impact was that you made upon a child, until well after they have left your home. Emma, a 7-year-old girl, went into foster care after her mom broke the femur of her father, who happened to be a Marine. This first grader stayed with us for just four months while dad was in the hospital recovering. The birth mom went to jail, convicted of attempted murder. I thought it was important for Emma to learn that "People aren't for hurting." Shaking my head "no," I asked her the question, "Is your mommy a bad person?" Confused, Emma said, "No." "Did mommy know what to do with her anger?" I asked while shaking my head "no" again. "No," she said. "Do you think your daddy would have been hurt if mommy knew what to do with her anger?" I asked. "No." she said again, now looking like she was beginning to understand. "Do *you* want to know what to do with *your* anger?" I asked her. "Yes." Emma said. I brought out a "bopper," a plastic bat with foam around it. We took turns hitting the tile floor, verbalizing all the things that are unfair. She knew what made her mad. "I miss my teacher!" Emma said, while she smacked the bat repeatedly on the floor. "It's not fair I got taken away from my Daddy!" she said, as she kept hitting. Then she picked up both boppers and started using them at the same time. "My Daddy's not for hurting!" she said, as she hit the floor the hardest. She paused for a moment to ask if I would take pictures of her, so she could always remember it. Aiming my camera at her, she began hitting the floor again with the boppers for over an hour. I used a whole roll of film taking pictures of her. Nearly two years after she reunified with her father, and now in third grade, Emma called to say "hi," and tell us her good news. She was bursting with excitement and could hardly contain herself. "Guess what?" she said, leaving no time to guess, and barely enough time to answer. "I got elected to the 'Peace Patrol' at my school and I get to carry a *real* 'Peace Patrol' clipboard, and I get to wear a *real* 'Peace Patrol' vest, and anyway, these two boys were fighting and I went up to them and told them that *'People aren't for hurting.'* - Do you remember teaching me that??" Tears of joy came streaming down my face. Emma could have easily grown up to be an abusive woman, just like her mom, and instead, she is serving on the 'Peace Patrol!' Amazing! God doesn't call the qualified, He qualifies the called.

For Emma:
"You are the light of the world.
A city that is set on a hill cannot be hidden.
Nor do they light a lamp and put it under a basket,
but on a lamp stand,
and it gives light to all who are in the house.
Let your light so shine before men,
that they may see your good works
and glorify your Father in heaven."
Matthew 5:14-16 (NKJV)

BEN

Ben was a curious little 4-1/2 year-old boy who was born drug-addicted, then abandoned at a very early age. He had brown straight hair, round-framed glasses and big eyes, and wanted to be physically close to me no matter what I was doing. One afternoon, I was cooking a big dinner and had several pots on the stove. When at the cutting board, I watched as Ben started to wander over near the stove to see what was going on there. "Stay away from there, okay?" I said to him. He just looked at me. "Stay away from the stove, Ben." I said more specifically, wondering if he knew that it was hot. "Do you know why I want you to stay away from there?" I asked. "Staff only??" he said. "Huh?" I said, not understanding. "*Staff only??*" Ben repeated. This "Staff Only" rule was all he knew having lived in an orphanage since he was 18-months-old.

There are many children today, growing up in an institution - either an orphanage, a group home or otherwise because of the lack of licensed foster homes. In general, when children come from an orphanage or group home, they act out and seem to be more "shut down" emotionally. Perhaps many of their feelings have been shoved away to allow their primary focus to be on survival. It is extremely rare to hear a name of one of their many caregivers. As in Ben's situation, every person was simply named, "Staff." These children *do* have their basic needs met, but miss out on so much by not being in a home. They experience staff changes and children coming and going frequently, often aren't able to be in a normal school setting, and there is no having friends over, climbing a tree in your backyard, or sneaking downstairs to get some cookies and milk. There are no sleepovers, helping prepare the family meal, or taking a karate class. The children can't go to a friend's house, stay up late and watch a movie all curled up on the couch with the family, or come home from school to freshly baked cookies. There is no parent to help out in the classroom, drive on a fieldtrip or establish a relationship with the teacher. There is no soak in a bubble bath after a tough visit with a birth parent, or sitting down for dinner and getting to process your day. These institutions, while protecting a child from being abused, may compound the effects of loneliness and rejection that the child experiences as a result of being in the system. While arguably better than the dreadful foster homes we have all heard about, an institution simply lacks the depth of bonding, learning, and trust that occurs within a healthy, loving foster home. Dear God, You can move mountains! Where there are abused and neglected children, there needs to be foster *homes* available for them. The children deserve a refuge, a place to heal. You are not a God that looks the other way. Please lay a burden on people everywhere to open their homes and their hearts for these, *Your* children. I will never stop praying for their needs to be met. In Your holy name I pray, Amen.

"Presence is more than just being there."
Malcolm S. Forbes

DAHLIA

I got a call about a taking a little girl named Dahlia who was a month shy of turning 3-years-old, and would be ready for discharge from the hospital in a couple weeks. She had been in the hospital for three months, after her hands and feet were plunged into boiling water and burned. When she fought against her hands going in, she caused the water to splash on her face as well. The social worker said Dahlia was a very mad girl and recommended that if we were to take her into our home, I first ought to plan on visiting her at the hospital several times, to get to know her, and get to know the daily routine of changing her bandages. It was a week until my birthday, and I hadn't come up with anything special to do yet, other than to go out to dinner. All of the sudden, it came to me. I would go visit Dahlia for the first time on my birthday. I told anyone and everyone who wanted to buy a gift for me, to please get something suitable for a 3-year-old! It was great. I got a *My Little Pony* with a brush, bubbles, coloring books and colors, a dolly, a stuffed animal, a couple Beanie Babies, a few books, a little squishy ball and some other toys. After my birthday dinner, I rushed to the downtown hospital where Dahlia was. I entered her unit, and from all the way down the hall, heard a child screaming. After checking in with the nurse, and while waiting for her to copy my ID, I quietly asked, "Is that child going to be okay?" Taking a deep breath, the nurse looked up briefly and said, "You'll see in a minute - *That* is the patient you came to visit!" I walked down the long hallway, toward the screaming. I entered Dahlia's room, and she looked at me and stopped screaming briefly. Then, as I came near her, she began to scream even louder. She was lying in a crib that resembled a cage. Her hands and feet were wrapped with bandages, and her eyes showed the magnitude of pain she was in. Thinking it might distract her, I showed her the large gift bag filled with unwrapped presents and told her I brought her some things. I took the pony out first, and carefully set it on top of the crib where she could see it. She screamed, "I *hate* you! You're *stupid*!!" Whoa, I thought. Then I got the brush out, and brushed the pony's mane and tail. I could tell she was interested, so I put both in her crib. With her hands wrapped like clubs, Dahlia couldn't hold the brush, but she managed to grab hold of the pony. Right as she got it she yelled, "*I hate you! I hate you!!* You're *STUPID!*" I didn't really react, other than turn away momentarily. Then I could see she was trying to get a glimpse into the bag. I took several things out and put them all around the plain, color-less room. I hung the stuffed animal on her IV stand, as she watched like a hawk. She grunted when I put a Beanie Baby down near her feet. I picked it up and put it next to her side. She yelled again, and this time I looked away, but gently stroked her forehead and hair. She was burning up! I went right to the nurse and after telling her, she said, "I know, I know, Dahlia is *so* underweight, that I *can't* give her nearly the medication she needs. I have to give it to her based on her weight." It dawned on me, that there was really no way to keep her out of pain. No wonder she was yelling. I went back in the room and she grunted again. I came closer, not making eye contact, which clearly made her feel threatened. Instead I started humming and went up and stroked Dahlia's head and hair over and over. A few times she started to dose off, then woke up yelling, "I *hate* you! *Shut up!*" I kept humming though, and she finally fell asleep. Every time I stopped stroking her head, Dahlia woke up, until finally, almost an hour later, she appeared to stay asleep. I kept humming as I managed to close and latch the crib. I slithered down to the floor and crawled across the room to grab my stuff. Then I turned around, still humming and crawling, and heading for the door to leave. I was almost at the threshold and I heard this little soft voice saying, "I hode (hold) you?" Then a little louder, "I *hode* you??" It was Dahlia. I came back in, and stayed almost an entire hour longer, humming and stroking her forehead and head with my nice, cool hands. Evan Esar said, "You can't do anything about the length of your life, but you can do something about its width and depth." I will never forget Dahlia, or how meaningful our very first visit was.

"Darkness cannot drive out darkness;
only light can do that.
Hate cannot drive out hate; only love can do that."
Dr. Martin Luther King, Jr.

DREW

Drew was a hyper-vigilant, caring, funny kid with dark hair and blue eyes. Even though he was in special education and functioning a few grade levels behind in school, he was 11-years-old, going on twenty-five, as far as street smarts go. While I drove, Drew pointed out the window and said, "I used to live there!!" and "Oh! - I used to live there!!" and being that fibbing is pretty common among foster children, it took a while to figure out that what he was saying was the truth. He actually *had* lived at several different locations. In one day alone, Drew pointed out a minimum of five or six places where he claimed to live within about a ten-mile stretch of road, and when turning to look, I sometimes saw nothing more than a parking lot or open field. Drew sometimes got very quiet and depressed as he recalled having been homeless. It was now clear why he commented so many times how "nice" our modest little home was. As the days passed into weeks and we all got to know him, Drew shared many stories of how he managed to live without numerous items anybody would consider "necessities." It was then that whenever the thought of buying something for myself entered my mind, the desire to do so would suddenly go away, and "things," for the most part, seemed so unimportant. When people make sacrifices and do something of real value, their life cannot help but take on a whole new meaning. Dear God, thank you for Drew, who is so inspiring.

Thank you that when he felt weak and it would have been easier to quit, he kept going. Thank you for giving him the spirit of resourcefulness when he was hungry, homeless and suffering. My prayer is that with your boundless compassion, infinite patience and incredible love, Drew understands that with You, all things are possible.

"Do not grieve,
for the joy of the Lord is your strength."
Nehemiah 8:10

DEBBY

Debby was a bright little 6-year-old girl who came to us after numerous bouts of domestic violence had occurred at her house. Her social worker had just told Debby that her daddy had to take a class before he would be able to get her back. "A class about what?" Debby asked curiously. "It is called Domestic Violence. It teaches daddy's that they can do other things besides hit mommy's when they get mad." "Oh." she said. After the social worker left, Debby came to me and insisted, "My daddy didn't *hit* my mommy." "I thought you said your daddy *hurts* your mommy, then your mommy *cries* a lot?" I said. "Why would she cry then?" I asked. "Because he *spanks* her very hard in the stomach and on the arms and on her back. Mommy says when daddy stops drugs he won't spank her anymore." Debby felt responsible for what was going on with her parents. She had ongoing anxiety, and worried constantly about how to keep her family together. She had been repeatedly punished for "talking about the family's private business," and as much as she tried to stay quiet, she couldn't help but tell others what was happening. After explaining that God knew all the things that were going on, even the secrets that her parents were keeping, and that she didn't have to worry because God truly *could* handle everything, Debby seemed relieved. She wanted to pray often. She took God's promises seriously and she inspired all of us by the way she prayed. After several months of living with us and attending church every Sunday, she learned more about God's character. She memorized her first scripture, "God will never leave you nor forsake you." (Deuteronomy 31:6) By that time, her anxiety was completely gone and she was just getting to be a little girl. One night, after a long and spirit-filled prayer with Debby, she looked right into my eyes and said, "All I want, is to fall in love with God."

"Tell me who you love,
and I'll tell you who you are."
Creole proverb

DANIEL

Daniel, a 13, soon-to-be 14-year-old boy, was tall and slender, had a great smile, and was one of the most popular kids at his school, in spite of the fact that he was raised by a drug addict. When his mom's live-in boyfriend molested his 16-year-old sister, the kids were taken into the system because his mom refused to kick her boyfriend out. Too bad no one ever taught Daniel that *Drugs make people stupid.* Had he known that, he might not have taken the actions of his drug-addicted mom personally. Daniel came to our home, and had to change schools. His sister went to another foster home close to their old house. Daniel was especially friendly, making all of us feel at ease, initiating conversation with each family member, and even sharing the use of his game system with the other kids. He was quick to laugh, very cooperative, and took to the house rules easily. He had a very positive attitude and it was clear that his biggest concern was for his sister. Daniel's outlook, determination, strong will and academic success in school wasn't a reflection of any nurturing or support going on at home. It was his way of coping - trying to be "good." He thought if he were good enough, his mom would choose him over her boyfriend, and then his sister would be safe. Daniel's mother didn't choose her children, but Daniel's grandmother didn't hesitate to take both children into her home when she realized that her daughter wasn't planning on dumping the boyfriend. I don't know that at age 83, she thought she would ever raising two teenagers. Dear God, Thank you for Daniel and his love for his sister. Thank you that he cares about having a good attitude and striving to do well. Thank you for meeting the needs of Daniel and his sister through their grandmother. Please bless her with strength, endurance, and all she stands in need of all the days of her life! I praise your goodness and mercy. In Your holy name I pray, Amen.

> "The Lord is righteous in everything he does;
> he is filled with kindness.
> The Lord is close to all who call on him,
> yes, to all who call on him in truth.
> He grants the desires of those who fear him;
> he hears their cries for help and rescues them.
> The Lord protects all those who love him."
> **Psalm 145:17-20** (NLT)

KIERA

This sweet little 6-1/2 year-old girl, with mounds of soft light brown ringlets extending down to her shoulders, was physically beaten badly by her birth mom's live-in boyfriend. When meeting her, Kiera came across as frail and submissive. Her clothes were worn and extremely outdated. When Sunday morning came, she was eager to go to church, or at least, wear the new dress, sweater, shoes and tights I bought for her. After church, the pastor introduced himself, and gave Kiera a children's Bible. She was so excited, that the minute we got into the car, she opened it up and began to slowly read it aloud. "In the beginning, God created the earth and the sun..." She stopped and gasped, and sounding surprised said, "*Really?*" She continued. "He made the moon and the stars..." - another gasp! "*Really!*" Kiera said once again. As she finished reading that God made all the animals and plants that live on earth, then man and woman, she said, "*REALLY*!!!!!!" and with a huge smile said, "I'm so excited because I thought he just made *us*!!" Sometimes, I feel very alone in caring about the rights of, and services provided to foster children. Night after night, I pray for these children. One thing that breaks my heart is the condition of the American Christians. What happened to the personal rights for all, that made this nation so great? We are people of great privilege - a nation of people more able, more affluent, and freer to act than any other in all of history. Yet, most do not seem to comprehend this. In my personal dealings with people, they seem to be generous and spiritually gifted, so why then are Christian's as a whole so slow to respond to these children? When I stand before God and cry out, He encourages me to send a message out to men and women everywhere that these are His children, and there is a call that rests on this nation to do something, now.

"When foster care is seen as His work, not mine,
the burden is light, not heavy,
and the work is an incredible privilege, not a chore."
Heidi McLain

HUNTER

It was exciting as always knowing we were getting a newborn baby. Not able to go down to the hospital that day to pick him up myself, the social worker brought him to our home. I remember answering the front door, and seeing her holding a tiny baby in a powder blue receiving blanket. Little Hunter was asleep when she placed him in my arms, then left. I rocked him and just looked him over - his little up-stretched arms that barely extended to the top of his head, a small tuft of blonde hair, tiny hands, a button nose and perfect little lips. When he opened his eyes, he gave me a huge smile that he held for a long time. *That's not typical for a newborn!* I thought, as I grabbed the paperwork and glanced at his date of birth. This baby wasn't a couple weeks old, as he appeared to be; he was three *months* old! It said that he weighed seven pounds, but he looked smaller. Curious, I read on. Hunter was deemed "Failure to Thrive," because he had only gained four ounces since birth. Apparently, his parents, nearly always high on drugs, had neglected to feed him on a regular basis, and after several weeks Hunter would barely suck on a bottle, and refused to drink vigorously, as a baby his age normally would. One prayer at a time, one bottle at a time, gaining one ounce at a time, eventually Hunter more than doubled his weight! It brought a huge sense of relief to the once concerned doctors and social workers that looked on. Because of the huge hurdle Hunter was able to overcome, some friends deemed me the "Baby Whisperer." Even though I am very fond of that title, ultimately, I am a just a woman of God, who wants to make a difference in the lives of each of these children.

> "When my father and my mother forsake me,
> then the Lord will take care of me."
> **Psalm 27:10**

ASHLYN

Ashlyn was a tall, precocious 15-year-old ninth grader, who had her childhood stolen right out from under her. She had long, dark hair and light blue eyes. Being extremely flirtatious, she taunted my two teenage boys. Ashlyn came into the system because her mom didn't protect her from being molested by her uncle. This had been happening for the past eight years. To make it worse, what was taking place was no secret to her immediate family, and her aunt often told her she "asked for it." Ashlyn suffered terrible nightmares, and never woke feeling refreshed. She performed poorly in school and was bulimic. She had sex and love mixed up, and got attention from boys to boost her poor self-esteem. She was sneaky, stole things from each of us, and lied with a smile on her face. The root of the behaviors was in her past, but they were affecting her future. I felt incredibly power-less in doing anything to help her. After working with her for several weeks, we realized that it just wasn't working out to have Ashlyn live with us, and she needed to be moved to another home. We continued to pray for her after she left. It was so sad to see such a sweet and beautiful girl go through this. Herbert Ward was correct when he said, "Child abuse casts a shadow the length of a lifetime." Dear God, please go with Ashlyn. Surround her and protect her. Give her all the love she needs, and when she is able to make choices for herself, the desire to keep herself clean. She is just a child, Lord. Lead her, guide her, heal her, and restore her. I pray she will accept You as her personal Savior one day soon, and press into You all the days of her life! Amen.

> "Don't copy the behavior and customs of this world,
> but let God transform you into a new person by
> changing the way you think.
> Then you will learn to know God's will for you,
> which is good and pleasing and perfect."
> **Romans 12:2** (NLT)

JAKE

Jake was in foster care because his drug-addicted mom neglected him. He and his siblings, four older and two younger, looked after each other and survived in a two-bedroom apartment, often without their birth mom there for days. They lived off ramen noodles, and the older ones took turns missing school to take care of the youngest, a 2-year-old boy, still in diapers. A year before Jake came to live with us, he and his siblings were removed and placed in foster homes, and over the course of that year, each of his siblings were placed either with their dads' or other relatives. This was not the case for Jake. His dad did not want him. No one wanted him. Jake acted out, and got moved from foster home to foster home, until a couple became interested in adopting him. He was so excited at the possibility of having a family that wanted him. Sadly, after three months, the family changed their minds, and Jake came to live with us. There he was, a 10-year-old boy, left without a future, at least for now. He showed up with all of his belongings in an enormous duffle bag. At first glance, it all looked dirty, and smelled like cigarette smoke, so I took it right to the laundry room. After it was washed, it was time to assess what he actually had. Now, keep in mind, this was everything he owned. Sorting it out, I found that Jake had *one* pair of socks, *two* pair of underwear three sizes too small, several t-shirts, all of which were stained and torn; a few pairs of jeans all raggedy and worn, a key to his bike lock, a dime, and some flannel night pants way too small. Nearly everything was suitable for the garbage. We went to Wal-Mart the next day, and bought several nice shirts, new jeans, a few pairs of nice shorts, new shoes, toiletries, underwear and socks. It was fun to see the look on his face when he realized he got to choose what type of underwear he preferred, and even whether he wanted the popular "no-show" socks, ankle length ones, or even tube socks. Several times while we shopped, I caught him looking at price tags. Once, he said, "This is $14.83. Is that too much?" "$14.83, huh! Are you *worth* $14.83?" I asked him. He just stared at me. I smiled and asked him again, more intently, "Are *you worth* $14.83, Jake??" His eyes started to well up with tears, and he remained quiet. This time I asked him while nodding my head yes. *"Are you or are you not worth fourteen dollars and eighty three cents*!??!" I asked. He reluctantly answered in a question tone, "Y e s s s ? ?" *"Yes!"* I said. "You *are* worth that and *more, Jake!"* He looked at me, with his big brown eyes and tapped the shopping cart nervously. Then he looked over at another foster child who had been with us for almost two years. "I just feel so bad. I feel like you should be buying things for her too, not just me!" he said as he dropped his head down. Before I could answer, the other foster child patted him on the back and said, "It's *your* day, Jake! I already *had* my day! It's *your* day!" She smiled. "When I need anything, Heidi gets it for me, so don't worry!" He lifted his head and tears rolled down his cheeks. Jake softly said, "This is better than any Christmas I have *ever* had!"

> "We make a living by what we get,
> but we make a life by what we give."
> **Winston Churchill**

MAKAELA

It was a Saturday afternoon, and I was attending an all-day seminar entitled, "Confidentiality in the Foster Care System" when my cell phone rang. It was a placement coordinator, asking if I had an opening for a newborn baby girl named Makaela. This drug-exposed baby would be ready for discharge from the hospital the following morning, so there was plenty of time to prepare. When arriving at the hospital, the information from the seminar was still fresh in my mind, and the seriousness of the laws, rules and recommendations that protect the confidentiality of foster children had been clearly stated. After quietly introducing myself as the foster parent, so no one would hear, the nurse escorted me to Makaela, where I signed papers and changed her clothes, then put her into the car seat. She was adorable, with lots of dark hair and blue eyes. Her skin was fair, and she had a nice, round "C-section" head. After stepping into the elevator, many people said how beautiful my baby was, and because of the strictness of the confidentiality laws, I didn't dare tell anyone that I was her foster Mom. When a curious lady asked how old Makaela was, and I answered, "just two days," she pointed to my almost flat tummy and said loud enough for everyone to hear, "*Wow*! You look *so great* for *just* having a *baby*!!!" Smiling, I replied, "Thank you!" The feeling was *exhilarating*! Now I know, to make any good day even better, going out in public with a newborn and the inevitable comments that follow, are right up there with sipping an iced Americano at Starbucks.

"A cheerful heart is good medicine..."
Proverbs 17:22

ADRIAN

After witnessing his mom attempt suicide, Adrian, a fifth grade boy, was taken into foster care. This 10-year-old was pudgy and reminded me of 'Rolly,' one of the puppies in *101 Dalmatians*, who kept saying throughout the movie, "I'm *hungry* Mama. I'm *hungry*." It seemed that the only way he knew how to self-comfort was to eat. Who could blame him? Adrian had been through a lot and was traumatized. He behaved very unpredictably and at times seemed confused. It was obvious after supervising the first three phone calls with his mom, that their roles were completely reversed. *He* was the parent and *she* was the kid. Each call he would ask, "You okay, Ma?" and she would answer, "Uhh, kinda. Ya, well, I'll be fine I guess." leaving him so unsure, that he wanted to call to check on her every hour. One Saturday afternoon, I was cleaning my garage while Adrian and several other kids were out on the driveway shooting hoops, and riding bikes and skateboards. Adrian came in and sat down on my garage

34

floor, close to where I was working. While listening to him talk, I glanced down and saw him trying to cut his wrist with a tiny screw. "What are you doing?" I asked. Barely drawing even a drop of blood, he answered, "I am killing myself." I explained that if he were serious, then I technically needed to call 9-1-1. "You are not for hurting, Adrian." I said, as I took the screw from his hand. Telling him to take a few minutes to decide, I called the other kids in. Luckily, that particular day, he changed his mind, but there were several other instances where he repeated this behavior. Adrian, like most children in foster care, faced situations and problems unlike those of his friends, so living in a home with other foster children, was somewhat of an informal group therapy session in a way, giving him and the others the opportunity to share and learn from each other. In time, the feedback that Adrian received from the other children was life changing.

Someone who personally gave me invaluable advice when I was just 14 years of age, the well-known talk radio personality, Dr. Laura [Schlessinger] shares her opinion that parents, who have their own children at home, should *not* become foster parents. Over the years, hearing this has hurt my heart. I agree that as parents, our first responsibility is to the safety, welfare, and proper upbringing of our own children, and it is our duty to not put them in harm's way; however, sometimes the magnitude of a problem, especially when it involves helpless children, warrants taking some risk.

About 65 years ago, an estimated 1% of the Gentile population in Europe hid Jewish children in their homes. It was extremely dangerous, and whole towns were said to have been burned as punishment in countries with a long history of anti-Semitism. Their courage was tremendous. In spite of the *risk to their own families*, numerous Gentiles *still* hid Jewish children and many of the children they hid are alive today. There are some striking similarities between Jewish children *then*, and foster children *now*.

- The children were often moved from one home to another.
- The children were separated from their parents, and worried they might never see them again.
- In most instances the children and their "rescuers" had never met before.
- What motivated the rescuers to take them into their home was the desire to help an innocent child.
- By saving a child, they changed history.

Being a foster parent and allowing your own children to be part of a foster family can be a direction and call on your life from God, as it was, perhaps, to the Gentiles.

Not a surprise, some 80 % of child welfare cases involve drugs, and often the addicts have burned their bridges with family members to the extent that not many relatives are willing to step up to the plate and rescue these children, let alone raise them. Relatives are generally sick of dealing with the addict, and often aren't willing to lovingly provide the court mandated visits, or even supervise the phone calls between the child and their parent. Often, their anger and resentment for the birth parent is expressed in front of the child, leaving them wounded, and feeling guilty and alone. Resultant acting out and bad behavior often sends the child out of a relative's home, and back into a foster home, only adding to the devastation and feelings of rejection the child already has. Additionally, relatives as compared to licensed foster parents do not have the intense initial training, or the required yearly re-licensing hours to help them deal with the problems they are commonly faced with. In essence, the dysfunctional family patterns continue. My own children have been taught about sacrifice, and living a service-oriented life. They know we are changing the future and the lives of some unfortunate kids, one at a time. They understand that there is currently a huge need for licensed foster homes, and without them, the devastating reality is that many kids are growing up in orphanages. So, my plea to Dr. Laura, with all due respect, is to re-think her advice to the millions of wonderful listeners raising their own children, who after hearing her might have abandoned their heartfelt desire to serve humanity in this way. The abused and neglected children did nothing to deserve what happened to them, and have a right to live in a loving and safe environment, where they can learn from both adults and interactions with other children. Without this, there simply will not be the kind of healing and restoration that stops the perpetuation of child abuse, even on its most minimal level.

> "Our lives begin to end the day we become silent
> about things that matter."
> **Dr. Martin Luther King, Jr.**

As a side note, I want to express my admiration for Dr. Laura because she fearlessly delivers her opinions and advice with boldness and strength of conviction that positively effects the morals, values, decisions, choices and lives of millions. In regards to situations that involve children, Dr. Laura exercises wise judgment, has delicate perception and keen insight in realizing and protecting their worth. I share with fellow Dr. Laura fans words from John Fitzgerald Kennedy: As we express our gratitude, we must never forget that the highest appreciation is not to utter words, but to live by them.

NATALIE
Natalie was only 5-years-old. She had shoulder length hair and bangs that went across her eyes, often hiding tears

of a grieving heart. Her nose and cheeks were covered in freckles and she had a number of teeth missing. As cute as she was, she had been through a very tough ordeal involving drugs and domestic violence in her home. When she lived with us, Natalie would come looking for me many times a day feeling fearful. Prayer seemed to help, and she really liked it as well. This little Kindergartener was especially excited to hear stories and learn about our Savior. Over several weeks, Natalie was beginning to get who God was, and rest in Him. She now knew that He was in charge, and was watching over her. We prayed often, and her anxiety level diminished. One day after school, I pulled up to the curb and she hopped in the van looking a little pale. "What was your day like today, Natalie?" I asked. "*It was scary*!!" she answered. "There was domestic violence across the street from school, and someone had a gun, so all the kids had to stay inside the classroom!" she said. "And some of the kids even had to go potty in the *trashcan*!!" she added. Poor Natalie. I felt bad for her, and was glad she was safe. I was curious, after having prayed with her numerous times in the seven weeks she was with us, if she thought to pray while at school that day. I asked her, "Do you know what you can *always* do, in the event of a crisis if you are scared, and no one would even know you are doing it?" She looked confused. It dawned on me that Natalie might not know the meaning of the word, "crisis." "First let me ask you - Do you know what a *crisis* is?" I asked. She took a long time to answer, and then finally said, "Well, now I know who Jesus Cris-is." That was so precious! All I wanted to do was hug her. Dr. James Dobson said, "I believe the most valuable contribution a parent can make to his child, is to instill in him a genuine faith in God." -And that is true. The only real weapon that will ever effectively win the war against neglect, domestic violence, child abuse and drugs is the Gospel of Jesus Christ.

> "Those who know your name trust in you,
> for you, O Lord, do not abandon
> those who search for you."
> **Psalm 9:10 (NLT)**

JAMES

James, a tall and adorable 9-year-old boy, with big blue eyes and straight blonde hair, that as much as he wished it would have, never seemed to be able to conceal his rather large ears, had been with us for several months after his drug-addicted mom severely neglected him. James couldn't wait for his birthday to come. Two visits were scheduled with his birth mom that week - one on Tuesday the day *before* his birthday, and one on Thursday, the day *after* his birthday. On Tuesday, his mother brought nothing for him. As the visit was ending, I made sure James was out of earshot and said to her, "Don't forget it is your son's birthday tomorrow - You *are* going to bring something for him Thursday, *right?*" She said she had no money. "Look," I said, "I don't care if you make a birthday card on a paper towel, and give him a pack of gum; you need to give him a card and a gift." When we returned for the Thursday visit, she handed him a home-made card on a paper towel, and a pack of Juicy Fruit gum. I thought it was pathetic, but said nothing, because it wasn't my place and James seemed happy. A child who had once suffered physical abuse and neglect that affected nearly every aspect of his life, James overcame enormous obstacles with his positive attitude, courage, determination and persistence to succeed. He stayed with us for almost another year. When it came time to leave, I was helping him pack up all of his belongings and opened a drawer, only to find the card and the pack of gum, unopened. "Oh wow!" I said, "...remember this?" James smiled, "Yes. It was the first birthday present I ever got from my mom - That's why I saved it!"

> "We could never learn to be brave and patient
> if there were only joy in the world."
> **Helen Keller**

LACIE

One day, my daughter Amanda, then in the 4th grade, asked to have a friend come home with us after school for a play date. "Sure!" I said. The next day, Amanda brought home Lacie. On their own, they chose several activities to keep them entertained. Twenty minutes later, Lacie was standing right behind me, not saying a word. "Do you need anything?" I asked her. "Nope." she said. "Oh," I said, as I starting walking back toward my daughter's room. "Let's see what Amanda is doing." I left, and headed into another part of the house. About 30 minutes later, I turned around, and there was Lacie again! Again, I asked her if she needed anything, and when she didn't, I re-directed her to where they were playing. The third time it happened, I realized it was something child psychologists called, "clingy behavior." If I remembered correctly, the children that exhibited it, had usually been abused in some way. I thought it was interesting. The next day, Amanda was invited to go to Lacie's house. I told her it was fine, I would just want to meet her parents. "Oh. She doesn't *have* parents. She has *foster* parents." Amanda said, matter-of-factly. Now, I was re-thinking the clingy behavior and it was making more sense. The next day, we went over to Lacie's house after school. Walking through the apartment complex and finally finding apartment #7, we gave the tall narrow window next to the door a good knock. *"COME IN!!!!!!!!!!"* I heard a man yell, in a gruff voice. The hairs stood up on the back of my neck as we checked to see if we were in the right place. We were. I opened the torn screen, then pushed in the partially opened door, and said to the large man sitting on the couch, sipping a beer, "Hi. I am Heidi and I guess Amanda and Lacie were going to play together today." He set his beer down, looked toward the staircase and yelled, *"Lacie!! Get the hell down here!!"* Down the stairs she came, but with her hands clenched in fists, arms stiff at her sides, and her eyes so wide open that you could see the white all the way around the iris. I was shaking, thinking, *She's scared of him! She's scared of him!* We left right away, and I will never forget the impression that left on my heart. The entire next day, I fought the idea of becoming a foster parent. I didn't think I would be *enough* - after all, it was just me, no dad. Plus, I knew there was no way to help Lacie anyway. On the other hand, I had an extra cozy bed at my house, and I knew our home had enough love. I prayed about it and didn't really trust the confirmation to go ahead with it that I got initially, but to be obedient to God, I went ahead and started the classes that began the licensing process, and thus was my entry into becoming a foster parent. Down the road, I noticed, that being a care-giver for a foster child is somewhat of a love gift, better yet, a *calling*. And when people see me with a bunch of happy, well behaved kids, and finally ask because they can't take it anymore, "Are *all* these kids *yours*??" I say with a smile, "Well, they are for *now*!" I suppose they most likely figure out that I am a foster parent, and inevitably honor what I am doing, at least to some extent, because I have heard numerous times, "God is *really* going to bless you!!" I always laugh a little, because I know something they couldn't possibly know. It's fun to say back, "It's *too late*! - He *already* has!" And it's true; God has already blessed my family *and* me in so many ways. Even though it is contrary to what much of the world believes, I know the biggest rewards in life come from sacrifice, service, and from centering yourself in God's will. I *love* love, and a world of love, makes a world of difference.

"Love comforteth like sunshine after rain."
William Shakespeare

KRISTEN & BRADLEY

Waiting to get my very first foster child, the phone finally rang - They had a baby girl, born methamphetamine addicted, with a fully collapsed right lung, a partially collapsed left lung, pneumonia and colic. This was a sick baby that now, after five weeks in the hospital, was finally ready for discharge. She was just what I prepared and asked for - A medically fragile, drug-exposed baby girl. "There is just one catch," the placement coordinator said. "...the baby has a 23-month-old brother, and we'd *really* like to keep them together." Realizing that I wasn't really prepared for an almost two-year-old boy, I decided to pray about it, and asked her to call back in an hour. I brought it to God, and asked Him to confirm whether *that* particular child belonged in *our* home. So insecure, I asked if He could please make His answer like a billboard in my heart, with red lettering, underlined, in bold print and highlighted. I prayed the answer would be obvious; I wanted to be sure. This was His child. Here is how my prayer was honored: The placement coordinator called back, and I asked if she could please give more information about the baby girl and her brother. She responded, "Well.... Her name is Kristen and his name is *BRRAAAADDLLEEYY*!" A divine coincidence, perhaps; my *own* kids names are Amanda, Christopher and *Bradley*! That was the confirmation needed. "Little Bradley" as we called him, was *in*, and that style of praying - asking God to show us His will for these children, worked beautifully. I will never forget that God loves these children more than I do, cares about each detail of their lives, and when we are still and seek *His* will not our own, the blessings are abundant joy and great happiness.

"Be still, and know that I *am* God..."
Psalm 46:10

JILLIAN

Jillian came to us looking like she hadn't been bathed in a month. She had long, dirty nails, stringy blonde un-brushed hair, and clothes that were way too small and smelled like urine. This little 6-year-old girl constantly complained that her tummy hurt. Jillian came into the system after her dad went to jail and step mom just wasn't able to make it on the streets. Both parents were drug addicts, and their lifestyle before dad went to jail consisted of pan handling, going from scuzzy motel to scuzzy motel, using drugs, and surviving from one day to the next. Jillian hadn't been to school in a few months. She was extremely bright, not shy at all, and never hesitated to share her opinion. Whenever I served her anything to eat, she shrugged her shoulders, pushed the food away and flat out refused to eat. Finally on day three, after being given a turkey and cheese sandwich and a cut up apple for lunch, and *not* being too happy about this, Jillian told me in no uncertain terms, "You and I need to go to the store so I can show you what *I* eat. I don't have breakfast or lunch, but I eat noodles called "ramen" for dinner *every* night. I am going to need some of those." Because of her extremely strong will, I felt I had to at least give her *some* of these noodles, even though they lacked nutrition for the most part. After many months and the almost constant gentle requests that she try new foods, Jillian begrudgingly began to eat more than just ramen noodles, but not without a fight. She vomited broccoli right at the dinner table, picked everything off pizza until only the crust remained, refused to have milk with her cereal, and was constantly spitting food into her napkin. Routinely, we asked her how her tummy felt just after trying something new. She would either say, "It feels good." or "It hurts." She had been living with us for 10

43

months and to everyone's surprise, one night she eagerly sat down to the dinner table for chicken enchiladas, rice, beans, and a salad. After a few bites, one of the kids asked her how her tummy felt. "Good!" she said with a smile. Jillian then laughed and said, "It feels *so good* to feel *so good!*" After enduring what seemed like an eternity through all the many meals with Jillian, and as a family experiencing the pain, strain, striving and effort; battles, diligence, drive and push; the stress, the struggle, the sweat, and the toil; we *all* felt such a *huge* sense of accomplishment; Jillian was happily eating a meal! We all rejoiced!

> "It's not that I'm so smart,
> it's just that I stay with problems longer."
> **Albert Einstein**

TREVIN

When I first met this 9-year-old boy Trevin, I noticed his dark hair, ears that stuck straight out, and big brown eyes that were welled up with tears. My first words to him were, "You okay, Trevin? You look like you are going to cry." "Are you gonna gimmie sumthin' to cry *about*?" he asked, as his eyes seemed to get even bigger. Not a surprise, Trevin had been physically abused most of his life. Knowing he had a history of acting out and bad behavior, I watched and even anticipated it, but week after week he continued to try each day to follow the rules, and do nothing he thought was wrong. One of my ideas on raising children is to let them overhear you saying wonderful things about them. Running into a friend, I introduced Trevin, and then whispered to her loud enough for him to hear, "Trevin is *absolutely* one of the most *well-behaved* boys I have *ever* known!!!" His face just lit up with a huge smile as he looked up to me and said, "And *you* are one of the most well-behaved *grown-up's I* have ever known!!" Reaching out and blessing a child, inevitably we end up being blessed ourselves. Lord, thank you for not forgetting Trevin, and for having a unique plan for his life. Thank you that you always know what you are doing. Thank you for the many foster parents that are listening, comforting and giving unconditional love to their foster children. Please continue to give each of us creative ways to communicate with them. In Your precious name I pray, Amen.

"Don't just pretend to love others. Really love them.
Hate what is wrong. Hold tightly to what is good."
Romans 12:9 (NLT)

GRACE

There I was, in downtown San Diego having dinner one evening, when I got a call asking if I could take a baby girl, not yet two-days-old, who needed a foster home that evening. The placement coordinator explained, "She is a 'preemie,' born heroin and meth (methamphetamine) addicted, and has pretty severe tremors from drug withdrawals. Oh, and she is HIV positive, and we already have her on the drug AZT." Scurrying out of the restaurant, I stood in the parking lot, waiting for the valet to bring my car, and thought for a fleeting moment about the challenges ahead, but couldn't help feel the excitement. I wanted to see what Grace looked like, and hold her in my arms. On the way to the hospital, it dawned on me that it was very unusual to get a call when I did. Usually they know the day before a baby is to be discharged. Praying as I arrived at the hospital, I checked in, and signed the papers. As the nurse walked us toward the nursery, she explained why the call came so late in the day. She said, "Well, there was another foster parent here earlier this afternoon, and when I began to give her the precautions in caring for an HIV positive baby, she literally walked backward out of the nursery saying, 'Sorry! - I can't do this!'" It amazed me. There is no blame or judgment; it is just sad that there is still so much ignorance today surrounding HIV. I was happy to have the opportunity to love and care for Grace! As she was placed in my arms, I suddenly felt a burden for her that was so strong that I had to sit down. I knew I was feeling the burden of love that God feels for these children. My heart was pounding, and my eyes filled with tears as I watched Grace's jaw and both of her arms tremor. What an amazing beginning to her little life. With all the challenges and defeats, hurdles and victories we overcame together through the grace of *God*, she quickly wiggled her way into my heart. She was a *champion!* Her will to live was inspirational. Grace struggled against terrible tremors that made it impossible for her lips to purse around a nipple, and suck down her formula. Instead it would drip down the sides of her tiny mouth. As a last ditch effort to get some nutrition into her, I sat with Grace on my lap, and used an eyedropper to drip warm formula down the inside of her cheek. She was very patient at feedings that took over an hour, and there was nothing better than to see her looking satiated. Although she continued to tremor until she was almost 13-months-old, her mouth became strong enough to suck out of a bottle when she was 4-1/2-months-old. About that time, she was retested and found to have sero-converted to HIV negative. *Nothing* is impossible with God. What a testimony to His power!

> "Finally, be strong in the Lord
> and in his mighty power."
> **Ephesians 6:10**

ISAIAH

Isaiah was back in the system for the third time after his mom was thrown in jail for using drugs. He was almost 10-years-old, but still had a baby face. He was so cute. His skin was darker than I had ever seen, and he was a little overweight with a pudgy tummy. Isaiah wore glasses with tape on the area at the bridge of the nose, and didn't have enough self-confidence to make much eye contact. He was my first "special ed" kid (of many) and his soft, low, scratchy voice just melted me. I had recently completed the addition of a room to our house, prompted by hearing about the two siblings of my last boy. Those three children, ages 4, 5, and 9, were left on their own completely, and barely survived. I would have given anything to have the extra room in my house at that time to take all three. Now, it was three months later, and Isaiah and I were putting the finishing touches on that extra room we had wanted so badly. Nice new bedding adorned the two twin beds, and we were in the process of covering the ceiling with glow-in-the-dark stars. Isaiah was helping by handing them up to me, while I stood on a ladder. "*Oh my gosh!*" I said. "What, Miss Heidi?" he asked. "I just realized something. Even if I *do* have two more beds, I can't take two more children - I don't have the room in my van!" My heart sunk over the disappointing realization. Just then, Isaiah's face lit up, and with a half smile he said, "Miss Heidi, I saw a show on TV called, 'CRIBS,' and they had a limo, and I promise it could hold all of us!" He paused a moment before asking nicely, "Could we please get one?" He was funny. Astonished, I had to admit, it was a great idea! And it would certainly be more fun than getting one of those 18-passenger cargo vans! Not long after all the kids were tucked into their nice cozy beds for the night, the internet helped locate a guy about 30 miles away selling the last of his used fleet. He had a Lincoln Towncar Executive Krystal Edition limo for sale. Thinking it would be perfect, we all took a test drive the following day after school. The nice owner, Paul, asked, "Will you be running a business?" "Nope," I said. "I am in the business of *kids*!" Nervously, he watched as all the children piled in the back of the limousine, and I hooked in the car seats for the little ones. We had a great test drive. It felt surreal! The next day, while the kids were in school, I went back and made him an offer; he accepted, and I drove back home just in time to pick Isaiah up from school.

When I first pulled up, school had just been dismissed and there was a sea of children everywhere. The limo quickly became the center of attention. Scanning and scanning trying to find Isaiah, I then realized, Duh! He'll see the limo! And he did. There he was, walking toward the parking lot from way out in the field. I watched a child walk up to him and say something, then Isaiah responded back and the other child walked off. Then another child walked up to Isaiah, said something, Isaiah responded, and that child too walked off. This happened several more times. Isaiah finally made it to the limo, and I hopped out to let him in, *celebrity style*. For Isaiah, who was continually harassed and bullied, this couldn't have been more fun. I got back in the driver's seat and asked, "What were those kids saying to you?" He looked at me and replied, "They were saying, 'That's *not* your limo, Isaiah!' and I said, 'Oh, *yes* it is!'" Then he slowly said in that low, almost monotone voice of his, "This limo sure does take the edge off the teasing, Miss Heidi." Smiling, I responded, "You deserve everything good, Isaiah."

> "It's good to have money
> and the things that money can buy,
> but it's good, too, to make sure you haven't lost the
> things that money can't buy."
> **George Horace Lorimer**

KATHERINE

A phone call came in, asking if I could take Katherine, a little 7-year-old girl. I was told over the phone that this second grader had been severely emotionally abused. She was short for her age, had an adorable smile, beautiful eyes, and without a doubt the hugest afro ever seen on a child. Her hair went out in every direction about seven or eight inches!

After picking her up and talking to her a while, Katherine said she had *never before* had her hair done! Right away, we went to Wal-Mart to get her all the things she needed, like clothes and shoes, panties and socks, toiletries and a backpack, and when I asked if there was anything else she needed, she asked, "Can you please buy me some pink lotion?" Without hesitation, I answered, "Sure!" and went a couple aisles over and grabbed some baby lotion off the shelf. "Is this okay?" I asked. Katherine just looked at the bottle. "Is *this* the kind of pink lotion you want?" I asked her again. She shook her head no. With much prodding, she explained that she actually gets something called 'Pink Lotion' in the hair aisle, and it is in a gray bottle, and she uses it to keep her hair soft. With her help, we found it, and everything else we needed to do her hair. We both went home so excited. It couldn't be *too* hard, could it? After Katherine went to sleep that night, I found myself reading the side of the *Pink Lotion* bottle. The next morning after breakfast, we got started. She was seated in a chair in front of a movie, while I made little parts everywhere, separating out groups of hair, smoothing pink lotion *in,* and tangles *out,* and doing this "twisty" thing that a friend showed me years earlier. At the bottom of every twist, I put a hair band, each with what looked like a pastel colored "dice" attached to it, that Katherine had excitedly picked out the day before. It looked great. When we were all finished, I announced that it was all done, and told her to go look in the mirror while I went into the kitchen to wash my hands. Katherine was beaming and had a smile on her face that will never be forgotten. In the next couple weeks, I would "catch" her in the bathroom, looking out of the corner of her eye in the mirror at herself, while shaking her head "no" over and over, so the little dice would swing back and forth, back and forth. *Clink-clank, clink-clank, clink-clank!* She couldn't wait to show her birth mom, and her visit was only a couple days after we did her hair. When we walked

49

in the room where the visit took place, she excitedly ran up to her mom, only to hear her say, "Katherine, you look so *fat!*"

"I will be glad and rejoice in your unfailing love,
for you have seen my troubles,
and you care about the anguish of my soul."
Psalm 31:7 (NLT)

AARON

Freckled-faced, 10-year-old Aaron was left to fend for himself when his birth mom went to jail for drugs. After a few days, he told his teacher and eventually was taken into foster care. When getting a new foster child, I always explain what "comfort food" is within the first day or two. I care about what they are used to eating, and which foods, healthy or not, are a comfort to them. In the last several years, it has been surprising to hear "hot Cheetos" as many times as I have, and unfortunately, the list also commonly includes boxed sugary cereals and ramen noodles - both cheap, "help yourself" meals common to neglected kids. Other comfort foods include Mac n' Cheese, candy, cakes and cookies, soda, chips and other foods which most of us would consider "junk." Although I teach children about eating right in an effort to make or keep their bodies healthy and strong, I usually give in to some of what they are used to. After explaining to Aaron about comfort foods, it was clear by the expression on his face, he knew exactly what I was talking about. As I readied my pen to write, I asked him, "What are *your* comfort foods, Aaron?" He smiled. "Oh, I have a lot of them!" he answered. "Shrimp, red snapper, lobster, filet mignon, that sparkling apple cider stuff, twice baked potatoes, pork ribs, Claim Jumper's chocolate cake...." I was writing and laughing a little, and even though I was caught off guard and a bit shocked, it was great to hear his marvelous list.

> "The sign on the door of opportunity reads PUSH."
> **Author Unknown**

JADEN

Jaden, a little 11-year-old girl, had been with us for over a year. She had long, shiny black hair and a soft, sweet spirit. She sat quietly at the dining room table, while I was making some new signs for the windows of our Foster Family Resale store. It was a Sunday morning, and normally we would be at church, but Jaden had come down with the flu the night before. We were talking about honesty, when she confessed that she had been holding on to a secret for a long time, and felt ashamed because of it. When I asked her if she wanted to share, Jaden began telling me that it wasn't just her mom's live-in boyfriend who hit her, but her mom as well. "I feel bad for lying all this time that it was only my mom's boyfriend. I *love* my mom, but that's why I don't *like* her too much." she said. She started crying, which was very unusual for her, and I went over next to her to hug her. She whispered, "I was embarrassed all this time that it was my mom. Plus, she only hit me for three reasons," she continued. Curious, I asked her, "What three reasons are those?" As the tears continued to roll down her face, Jaden answered, "She only hit me when I asked for help, when I told her I was afraid, and when I cried." "People aren't for hurting." I said to her, as I had many times before. Jaden reached her arms around me and gave me a long hug. She looked up with her long, wet eyelashes and said, "I feel so much better. I think I am going to go lie down now." When walking up the stairs she said, "Oh, and Heidi? .... Thanks for never hurting me." For all children, to be loved and to love is unmatchable. And thank you God that Jaden had the opportunity to experience that through speaking the truth, she could be free from the shame, and healed in the deepest corners of her soul.

"God will wipe away every tear from their eyes;
there shall be no more death, nor sorrow, nor crying.
There shall be no more pain,
for the former things have passed away."
Revelation 21:4 (NKJV)

LOGAN

Logan was a skinny, 10-year-old dirty blonde-haired boy with big, blue eyes. He was diagnosed with severe ADHD, and had been living with our family as a foster child for 1-1/2 years because his mom physically abused him. We fed him healthy foods, and bought a huge trampoline so he could jump off some of his excess energy. After just a few months, his doctor met with Logan and decided to take him off all his medications. Logan turned out to be a pretty awesome kid, who was getting ready to be reunified with his birth mom. One of the last things he said, as we were packing up his things was, "Thanks for never hitting me. Actually, thanks for never even yelling at me." The truth be told, Logan was easy to love. He blessed our family by being part of it. He helped all of us to remain child-like in our appreciation of life. Dear God, we thank you so deeply for Logan, for the love we have for him, for the opportunity You gave us to be with him, to teach him and to love him. Thank you that you take *his* care and the care of *all* your children seriously. I pray that he will know the importance of having You in his life. I pray when he is facing trials, that he turns to You. God, please give more people the desire and the willingness to become loving foster parents. Let them consider giving up something they are doing that is not productive, and does not glorify You, and pray for you to show them how they can

serve children. Serving children is such a rewarding investment in Your kingdom. In Jesus' name I pray, Amen.

> "You can't do everything at once,
> but you can do something at once."
> **Calvin Coolidge**

MADISON

5-month-old Madison was the first baby I had taken as a
result of domestic violence occurring in the home. She hadn't
been hit or physically injured. In fact, she was so healthy and
chubby looking, she didn't look abused in the least. Madison
had luscious rolls of fat you just wanted to squeeze, and the
nurse who checked her, said she was in the 95th percentile for
her weight! Madison was taken into foster care after social
services was notified by the police that there were many
calls out to the house because of her parents fighting. Social
services agreed that all the fighting was actually causing harm
to her. Had I not experienced it myself, it would be difficult
to believe. She *was* truly frightened. When I picked her up,
her eyes were wide, and she looked scared as she clung to
me. I put her in the car seat and we headed for home. It
took some time before Madison began to settle down. At the
very first visit, the 18-year-old mom said, "I really miss my
baby. I miss doing things with her and having her around."
She asked how Madison was doing and I explained that
she was still pretty uneasy and often scared. "When is she
scared?" the mom asked. "Well, she jumps when she hears
a loud noise, shakes when a door shuts, and even startles if I
enter the room suddenly. She still isn't content in the swing
or playing on the floor with toys." "Oh! That's because I
never did those things with her." the mom said. "We did
other things," she continued. "Like what?" I asked. "I used
to prop Madison up on the couch and let her watch movies."
"Hmmm," I responded. "Like what movies?" "Umm, the last

movies she watched were *Terminator* and *Terminator 2*, and, Oh! - *Saw*. And also *The Exorcism of Emily Rose*." she said. She was serious. She had little Madison watching horrifying movies, and didn't think anything of it. Curious, I asked, "Didn't she cry?" "Well, whenever she cried, I just gave her a bottle." the Mom answered. Wayne Dyer said, "When you judge another, you do not define them, you define yourself." I have always thought judgment brings defensiveness, and love brings change, so instead of judging this young mom, we just taught her how to take good care of Madison.

"When you extend yourself in kindness and spirit,
one to another, that comes back to you."
Oprah Winfrey

MICHELLE, MIKE and MATTHEW

Michelle, a 12-year-old girl, with dirty blonde hair and especially beautiful blue eyes, along with her two brothers, 10-year-old Mike and 7-year-old Matthew, came to us, just for a weekend, waiting for a relative to travel down from up North to take them. Their mother had abandoned them several years earlier, and their dad, who was raising them on his own, was arrested and taken to jail after a drug bust. Her two brothers seemed fine playing video games nearly all day and night with the other boys in the home, but Michelle was depressed and it seemed to be getting worse the second day. I had to think of something to help her. Getting my camera out, I asked if she would like to have her hair done, then do a special "photo shoot." She readily accepted. Michelle chose a "crown" French braid, which showed off her beautiful facial features. After being pampered a little bit, she got excited and wanted her picture to be taken in every pose, all around the house and backyard. Michelle insisted her picture be taken in the kitchen and living room, backyard, at the piano pretending to play, lying down and standing up, sitting in a beauty pose, and even some with a fan blowing on her face! When we were done, I went upstairs to download the pictures and print them out. I even had a little mini photo album to put them in. Some I printed out in black and white for effect. She was so excited. As we looked through them together, Michelle asked if she could keep the album. "Of course." I answered. "This was *so* fun!" she said. "What was the best part of it?" I asked her. "Well, this was the first time I ever really felt pretty!"

> "I will praise You, for I am fearfully
> *and* wonderfully made;
> Marvelous are Your works,
> And *that* my soul knows very well."
> **Psalm 139:14** (NKJV)

GINGER & BRUCE

Ginger, a fair-skinned four-year-old girl with dark brown shoulder length hair, and her 1-year-old brother, Bruce, who was barely walking, were placed with us after they were removed from their home because of physical and emotional abuse. At our house, they both had plenty of toys to play with. Often, when my back was turned, I would hear Bruce cry out suddenly. When I turned toward him, or came back into the room, Ginger would be speaking to him very sweetly, and say she didn't know why he was crying. One day, they were playing together, and Bruce had already cried out twice, so pretending I wasn't watching, I said to her, "I am going to take this laundry upstairs." I peered at them from the landing, halfway up the stairs, only to see Ginger tease Bruce with a big truck until he grabbed for it, then jerk it away, and hit him over the head with it. Shocked, I raced down the stairs, and asked her what happened. She said, "Bruce tried to take this truck away from me, and I had it first!" That afternoon, he was napping, and it was snack time. I made

Ginger a peanut butter and jelly sandwich, and cut it into a heart, her favorite shape. With her tiny hands, she was eating this heart-shaped sandwich, and I was wiping the crumbs off my counter when I asked her, "Ginger, why do you hurt your brother?" Her answer was surprising. "Because voices in my head tell me to do bad things." "Well, tell them '*NO! I won't* do bad things!'" I said. "I tried that, and it didn't work." she replied. I returned the sponge to the sink and sat down next to her. Speaking softly, but glaring straight into my eyes, Ginger said, "And those voices tell me to do *other* things too, like *kill* people, *good* people like *you!*" Dear God, today all Ginger has is me. I am only one person, but I know one person can make a difference, and if I can do that, I will be happy. I will love and comfort her; I will pray for her in boldness; but only You can heal her, and I pray for that in Jesus' name. Amen.

> "Neurosis is always a substitute
> for legitimate suffering."
> **Carl Gustav Jung**

"BABY BOY"

The Placement Coordinator called to ask if we could take a drug-exposed newborn, who was ready for discharge from the hospital. "What's his name?" I asked. "Baby boy." she answered. That's what they say when the parent refuses to name their baby. For several weeks, we called him that until his birth mom eventually named him Elijah. I called the social worker at the hospital and made arrangements to come get him. I had never gotten a baby from that particular hospital before, and was shocked when I was getting ready to leave, and they stopped me. The nurse said, "It's our policy for the mother and baby to ride out of the hospital in a wheelchair." I laughed, "But I am only his *foster mother!*" I whispered. "I know," she said, "but that's our policy!" I didn't argue.

She radioed someone to come. A nice gentleman showed up with a wheelchair, and after I sat down, he carefully placed the baby carrier on my lap. As he went over the threshold leaving the nursery, I shouted, as I winked at the nurses, "*Careful*! *My uterus*!" They smiled, shook their heads and even quietly laughed as the gentleman immediately apologized. He wheeled us down a long hallway, then into a huge elevator. Seconds later, at least a dozen people hopped in. At the center of attention, nearly everyone "ooo'd" and "aww'd." A nurse standing next to us said, "Your baby is so cute!" "Thanks" I replied, since, because of confidentiality laws, I couldn't say I was his foster parent. "He's so *tiny*! How much did he weigh?" another person asked. "I don't know." I said with a half-smile. Still another person asked, "Awww, what'd you name him?" "Ummm, *Baby Boy*!" Greg Anderson said, "When we are motivated by goals that have deep meaning, by dreams that need completion, by pure love that needs expressing, then we truly live life." This was the case in caring for Elijah.

> "I chose you when I planned creation."
> **Ephesians 1:11 (Paraphrased)**

ELLEN

Ellen was a 7-year-old second grader, who was absolutely adorable with her blonde hair and dimples, but all the fibbing she was doing had to stop! The main thing she lied about was sneaking food, especially sweets. It was completely understandable, since Ellen had just come from a living situation where she was not given enough food; but even still, her lying needed to stop. A couple of weeks earlier, after being caught red-handed, Ellen was told to ask me before having any sugar at all. When picking her up from school one day, I noticed her little mouth surrounded with what looked like the dark cookie part of an ice-cream sandwich. Concealing my smile, I told Ellen, "I am about to ask you a question, but before I even ask you, I want to remind you to *answer truthfully*, so you can feel *really good* about yourself." She immediately had a guilty look on her face. "What's the question?" Ellen quickly asked. I looked at her straight in the eyes, "Did you have any sugar today?" She thought for a good long while before answering. "Can I please lie *this* time and tell you the truth *next* time??"

> "Nothing I have ever done has given me more
> smiles, giggles, laughs
> and rewards than being a mother."
> **Heidi McLain**

THOMAS

Thomas was 11-years-old when he came to live with us. He was overweight and very tall for his age, had a learning disability, few social skills and absolutely no table manners. He chewed with his mouth open, used his fingers to push the food on to his fork, spilled on his shirt at nearly every meal, and sat slouched over with both arms on the table, almost hovering over his plate. He routinely gobbled down everything in front of him to get a second serving before the food was gone, and rarely checked to see if anyone else wanted more before he took the last of something. Knowing his history made it all make sense. Thomas had been poor and homeless and in the habit of dumpster diving for food each and every day of his life before coming to live in our home. He had missed years of school at a time, and any money he was able to get, he used to buy fast food. He knew exactly what was on each restaurant's dollar menu. He knew where every church was, at least the ones that offered a hot meal to the homeless. He knew all the buses and where they went, and wasn't afraid to ride them. Among all the glaring problems he had, none of which were his fault, something about this boy, with his fair skin and brown hair, cherry red chapped lips and soft brown eyes, stood out. From the very first to the very last meal he was served, for two years, seven months and two days, whether it was breakfast, lunch or dinner, and no matter if it was something very fancy or a simple stand-by meal, this boy, without fail, always said with sincerity as he was clearing his plate from the table, "Thank you *very much* for this meal, Heidi." Thomas truly appreciated all that was given to him. Just before he turned fourteen, he realized that his parents, both homeless drug addicts, did not do what they needed to do to get him back. He knew that my calling was to be a foster parent and that I did not plan to adopt him. He was faced with growing up in the system, and possibly going to an orphanage where only teens lived. The realization was devastating for both of us. We agreed to trust that God had a plan for him. A few weeks later, like many, many times before, Thomas was asked to go over to his friend Austin's house. When I pulled up, Austin's parents came out to greet us. They said they just heard I was a foster parent, and asked if I had any of my *own* children besides Thomas. I answered with much hesitation, "With all respect to confidentiality, Thomas *is* a foster child." They were shocked. The next morning, they called asking if I could somehow approach Thomas to find out if he might want to grow up with them. It wasn't hard to see that they were totally excited at the possibility of adopting him, and practically held their breath waiting to hear back. When I called to tell them that Thomas said yes, they immediately wanted to know everything they would need to do to adopt him. Now, living with them in a licensed foster-adopt home, with the goal of adoption, Thomas continues his sacred journey, knowing that God *does* answer prayers, and have a very special plan for his life.

"I will not leave you orphans; I will come to you."
John 14:18

MADELINE

Maddie was so severely abused, that after hearing her story, I honestly felt less than qualified to take her. They explained that she was so terrified, she had been crying continuously for nearly six hours. Maddie was physically abused, and left alone in an apartment for several days. In her situation, I would cry too; she was 2-years-old. My own feelings of inadequacy were keeping me from mustering up the courage to say yes to taking her. I prayed, *God! If you want Maddie in our home, lay it on my heart, and give me courage!* Feeling prompted to, I agreed to take her, but did not receive what I later understood to be my *real* call from God, until I first held Maddie in my arms. When I first looked in her eyes, it was evident life had taught her never to trust anyone. As I lifted her up, Maddie's little arms gripped around my neck, as she hesitantly surrendered the weight of her head, letting it rest on my shoulder. With my fingertips, I gently moved her tear soaked bangs out of her eyes, and placed my palm, gently on the back of her head. As I held her, I instinctively swayed back and forth, and an overwhelming feeling of gratitude filled my heart. There I was, in the center of His will for *my* life, babysitting for **God**!

"And whoever welcomes a little child like this in
my name welcomes me."
Matthew 18:5

MICHAEL

Michael was a 9-year-old boy, who was put into foster care because his birth mom was arrested and thrown in jail for selling drugs. The drug bust happened while Michael was at school, so a social worker came and removed him right out of his classroom. He had no idea what was happening and was devastated as someone, whom he perceived as a stranger, took him away. When we came to pick him up, Michael looked extremely scared. Walking out to the parking lot, I made an attempt to reassure him that we would be taking good care of him while they helped his mom. It was always exceedingly more fun to be going out to the car and ask the child, "Guess which car is ours?" when we were driving a limo. By Michael's reaction, you would have thought I'd taken him to Disneyland or something. He absolutely was beside himself. Bursting with happiness from that moment on, it was all Michael talked about. Ironically, we had taught each "new" child to enjoy the limo, but learn how to somewhat downplay its importance. Never brag or feel better than anyone because of it, and realize that "stuff," including the limo, is not love or safety or family or anything but "stuff," and it certainly doesn't buy happiness. Since everyone requests 'the limo story,' here it is: Thanks to a small settlement after a minor car accident, and a nice guy at a limo company who gave us a deal we couldn't pass up, we purchased a real, 10-passenger Lincoln Towncar Executive, Krystal Edition limousine. For several years, in addition to our van, we had the limo that could hold all of us. The inside of the back had a television, twinkle lights on the roof that changed color, leather interior that could be wiped down easily, a moon roof that thanks to God didn't work (Sorry kids!), coolers in the lit bar that became side-by-side toy boxes with every hand held game you could imagine, and my favorite feature - privacy *glass* and a privacy *screen* that with a touch of a button could go down or up, separating the front seat from the "cabin," as it was called. The children could listen to *their* music and even be somewhat loud, while I was able to calmly do the driving. Most importantly, we made some pretty awesome memories. In the six years that we had the limo, it was used to bring incredible joy to a whole bunch of children. At random times, for no particular reason, I would pick them up from school in it. They knew it was okay to offer their friends a ride home. It made running errands almost complaint free. The kids loved to be riding around town in it and enjoyed the attention. It also added extra joy on many different occasions like birthday's, promotions, graduations, school dances, first and last days of school and fieldtrips. We offered it for the transportation as part of prizes for school fundraisers, brought birth parents to and from visits with their children, and it made a child's attitude about going to the doctor or dentist worlds easier. Whenever I would stop at a gas station to fill up, people would try to rent it out, and I'd have to explain that it was our *family* car! One day, a man on the other side of the pump reached around and handed me his business card. He matter-of-factly asked that I call him to arrange the reservation of the limo. "Oh no," I said, "This is our *family* car." "*Really*?" he said, smiling. "Yeah, this is the car you drive when you have a lot of kids!" I explained. "Huh!" the guy said, shaking his head a little bit. "Well, *this* is the car you drive when you *don't* have *any* kids!" he said while chuckling. I peered around the pump to see a beautiful new Porsche convertible! We since sold the limo, but during all the years we had it, there was only had one parent who seriously accused us of purposefully getting it so that her child would never ever want to return home to her. That was Michael's mom!

> "You pray in your distress and in your need;
> would that you might pray also in the fullness of
> your joy and in your days of abundance."
> **Kahlil Gibran**

DAKOTA

Dakota, a very small-framed 7-year-old girl with red hair and freckles, carefully watched everyone's move from the moment she hopped into our van to come home with us. Right away, she kept track of when it was time to feed the baby and memorized the entire family's weekly schedule. She woke up at 5AM because she was used to having to get herself up and ready and out the door for school on her own, and she wouldn't stop checking up on everyone in the house to make sure each person was safe. Dakota and her parent's roles were completely reversed, and because of this, she became "parentified." Often children of drug addicts become this way. The addicts themselves often brag about their children being "extra responsible," when the reality is, that the child's actions are a result of neglect and fear, and fall under the category of survival behaviors. Dakota was the responsible one, and had to make sure her drug-addicted parents were doing the right thing. "Get up for work, Daddy!" "Mommy, you left the keys in the car!" "Mom! - Didn't you say you had to work at 3:00PM?" "Dad! You are smoking in bed again! That could cause a fire!" "Mom - You forgot to lock up." "Mom - Don't you have to pay the electric bill today or else the lights get shut off again?" "Wake up, Dad - You have court today!" This is a 7-year-old girl, and these are just *some* of the reminders Dakota gave to her parents. As you can imagine, she got lots of accolades from them for doing this, and even though these are unhealthy behaviors that shouldn't be continued while in foster care, just asking Dakota to *not* do them anymore wouldn't work. The responsibility she was used to taking on, would have to be replaced with something else she could feel good about, or she would soon suffer from depression and a sense that she no longer had value. At 7-years-old, Dakota didn't think twice about coming up to me with her dirty clothes, and asking where the washer was, completely prepared to do her own wash! She needed no assistance in getting ready for school, and didn't ask for help with her hair. No one had to tell her to do her homework, and on her first night with us, she offered to make dinner. *Seven* years old! One thing that she didn't like was how tired she felt most of the time. I would reassure her constantly that she could rest, and I would take care of everything. The wonderful thing was that even though it took quite some time to overcome, after a while, Dakota, like other "parentified" children, *did* relax, and happily jumped feet first into the role of being a child. She liked being released of responsibilities that belonged to adults! And she liked it so much, she often corrected her parents and other grown-ups when told, "Now, you be a good girl and help take care of your sister!" by saying confidently, after receiving a quick glance of reassurance, "That's not my job! *My* job is to be a *kid*!" It might have been the first time Dakota was ever allowed to act her age. It is nice to give children back the sense of self, and freedom to be a child, that often gets taken away through abuse, neglect and abandonment.

"Come to me, all you who are weary and burdened,
and I will give you rest."
Matthew 11:28

JOEY
Joey was a 10-year-old freckled faced boy, who came to us when his birth mom went to jail for stealing. When asked whether he knew why he was in foster care, Joey said, "I can take a guess - It's either because my mom stole something, or got caught with dope." He later said his mom routinely stole things to sell so she could buy drugs. Curious, I asked, "How do you know she steals things?" "Well," he said, "We don't even have a baby, and my mom takes an empty stroller to stores and makes me load it with things that she wants to steal." Soon after Joey came to live with us, we met his mom at McDonald's for an hour-long visit. One the way home, Joey made a comment about doing foster care for the money. "Why would you say that?" I asked. "My mom just told me,"

he answered. There are *always* people that do things for the wrong reasons. Here are the current monthly foster care rates, so no one ever has to ask a foster parent if they do it for the money. [Note: These are the rates in CA, some of the *highest* rates in the US] Ages: 0-4 - $446, 5-8 - $485, 9-11 - $519, 12-15 - $573, 16-18 - $627. The money is intended to be a *reimbursement* for the child's living expenses, not for *us* the caregiver, since we are actually volunteering to care for the child. If we weren't, we would be caring for a 0-4 year old for 61 cents per hour! If we take a closer look at the reimbursement rate for children, ages 0-4 years ($446/ month,) this amount is meant to pay for everything the baby or child needs in a month. All the diapers or Pull-up's, diaper rash cream, baby wash, lotions, shampoo, baby wipes, food and baby food, and things like pacifiers and over-the-counter medications. We are expected to already have a diaper bag, bottles, crib and bedding, changing table, baby swing, stroller, infant car seat, toddler car seat or booster seat, toys and any other baby supplies. It is supposed to cover the portion of living expenses normally incurred in a home, and even the gas to and from all the pediatric, doctor, dentist, and therapy visits, as well as visits with the parents and social workers. There is a clothing allowance of $100 twice a year, but if you have been shopping for clothes lately, it doesn't buy much for a growing child. If you still aren't convinced that foster care rates are deplorably low, call your local pound and find out what it would cost to kennel your puppy for a month. That's just feeding and kenneling them, and maybe a walk or two a day, not parenting them. I love animals but think kids deserve at least equal justice. According to an annual study by the USDA, the average cost for a middle-income family to raise a child born in 2007, until age 18, is estimated at a staggering $204,060. And that doesn't even include infla- tion or college costs. This factors out to approximately $945/ month per child, almost twice that of what foster families are reimbursed, yet foster families are still paying for living expenses, food, clothing, cable, telephone, gas, electric, water, trash bills and mortgages. I believe that there is not a more *basic responsibility* of a government than to protect and provide for those who cannot do so for themselves: namely children. The failure of government in this instance, to secure the well being of foster children, is beyond excuse; it is nauseating.

> "Government, obviously,
> cannot fill a child's emotional needs.
> Nor can it fill his spiritual and moral needs.
> Government is not a father or mother. Government
> has never raised a child, and it never will."
> **William Bennett**

KATHLEEN

Kathleen's story is such an important one to share. I want every person who knows of a child trying to grow up with an alcoholic parent to pay close attention to the words I have written here because they are coming straight from an innocent 9-year-old. When Kathleen was sharing, I happened to be writing this book, so I had paper and a pen on my lap, and wrote almost everything she said *verbatim*. Sweet Kathleen, with shiny light brown hair and chubby cheeks was put into the system when her mother was arrested for drunk driving and assaulting a police officer. The incident happened in front of her, and you would think that she would be very upset, but she was remarkably calm. I kept a close eye on her, thinking she'd be having a crying "meltdown" or at minimum be asking if we could contact her mom, but it didn't happen. Instead, Kathleen wanted to take a swim in the pool, play with our dog, find out about the new school she would be attending, and play in her bedroom. After school the following day, the kids and I were out in the backyard swimming and relaxing. Kathleen was sitting sideways in the lounge chair next to me, like a rag doll with both legs draped over the arm of the chair when she said in a happy voice, "I just *love* being here! Can I *please* stay for a *really* long time?" Answering with a question, I said, "Why is that?" "Well, *because*," she said with conviction, "I have been waiting for this for a *very long time!*" She continued, "I don't want to give my mom another chance. *Every* time she does something bad, she makes the excuse it is because of *alcohol*, but she *won't* stop drinking. She tells me and my brother [sic] not to lie, and *she* lies all the time, and when she is mean to me, she forgets by the next day. Plus, she doesn't even pay attention to me anymore. All she mostly talks about is things from a long time ago. She doesn't even know what I like now. I used to like *Dora the Explorer* when I was five, and now I am already *nine,* and I don't even like that show anymore. She doesn't know that I like Hannah Montana now." [Because I was so intent on writing every word she said, I said almost nothing to her, but instead looked up occasionally and nodded my head. She just kept on talking, so I just kept on writing. It was, for the most part, a monologue.] "My mom doesn't know if something is bugging me, and never asks me if I need anything like she used to when I was little. At our school assembly last Friday, I got an award and she wasn't even there. She told my teacher she was sick, and she wouldn't have been sick if she hadn't gotten so drunk the night before. She thinks I am *stupid!* Other parents help out at school, and when I was in first grade I used to want *her* to, but now, even when she comes to pick me up after school, she embarrasses me. I used to tell her to stop being so late to pick me up, but now I think it is better because then none of my friends see her. She has even yelled at the people who work in the school office and they had to call the cops once. After school when I need help with my homework, she is always sleeping, so I just ask my friends instead of her. She doesn't even know. Sometimes she talks about weird stuff and stumbles around our house because she is so drunk. The worst thing she did at my house was take a bottle of wine into the hot tub and drank the whole thing by herself. She was yelling for me to help her and when I came outside, she was passed out. She wouldn't wake up, so I had to try and hold her arms and shoulders so she wouldn't go under water and drown. The next day I was thinking she would say sorry, but she didn't even remember. In fact, she was actually late taking me to school that morning. One day last year, I missed our best fieldtrip to Sea World because she was so late taking me to school that day. I am mad at her but can't tell her because last time I did, she got drunker and broke a mirror in our hallway and I had to clean it up so my younger brother wouldn't get cut. I am glad the cops took her away because I am pretty sure you aren't allowed to drink alcohol in jail. Now maybe I can relax."

My two cents: Drug and alcohol use can *become* a problem, but it starts off as a *perceived solution* to another problem. Addicts don't have a *disease*, but they *do* have a *sickness*. Using drugs or alcohol causes parents to neglect the needs of their children. Making a "substance" the excuse for bad behaviors, teaches children to do the same and *not* take responsibility for their own actions. Even when addicts get into drug or alcohol treatment programs, the children are sometimes *still* neglected because it often continues to be all about the parent. "I am going to my program." "Mommy has to go to a meeting!" "Look at this - Daddy got another ring for his keychain!" "Aren't you proud of Mommy for graduating her program??" The attitude is like, 'celebrate me' and once again, it is all about *them*, which continues the pattern of child neglect. I am not saying recovery is bad, but when you are putting the focus on you, it is *not* on the child. Is your little girl missing Girl Scout's or not getting help with her homework because you are tied up on the phone with your sponsor, or have another N.A. meeting to go to? Are you too busy focusing on how many days of sobriety you can celebrate, while forgetting that your son has outgrown his clothes, or he like his friends, wants you to help out in his classroom? Malaria is a disease, not addiction. No disease makes a person steal to go get drugs and put a meth pipe up to their mouth and smoke it, or drink alcohol until they are drunk. These children have been through enough. Take responsibility, get help and do your best to catch up on all that you lost touch with. Utilize a good therapist to work on your emotional development that was stunted all the years you used, but most of all, please get to know your kids and make it all about *them*. They are only children once. One final thought and plea: I love caring for your beautiful children, but it is their birthright to have *you* raise them, if you are able. There is no rewind button in life, so I encourage you - get it together, get your kids back, do the right thing, and give your children the childhood they deserve. I am rooting for you!

"For nothing is impossible with God."
Luke 1:37

JOAQUIN

Joaquin was a little Hispanic boy with a shaved head and big brown, expressive eyes. He was short for his age, but made up for it in speed. Kindergarten gave him something to do, and his little round glasses didn't keep him from participating in any sports or other activities. At only 5-1/2-years-old, Joaquin had already experienced two deaths in his immediate family due to gang violence. His mother was in jail and his father was in prison, both incarcerated for drugs, gang violence and various other crimes. When I first got Joaquin, he seemed unscathed by it all. He ran around, played, ate and slept well, and was, for the most part, obedient. One day, we were all sitting in the van out in the driveway, waiting for a case aid to drop off a child after his visit, so we could leave to have dinner with friends. My son and I were in the front seats; two babies in their car seats were in the middle row of the van, and Joaquin was seated in the back row. The case aid pulled up, and I got out of the van to greet the other child. Less than a minute later, my son jumped out of the car yelling, *"Mom!! Joaquin is hitting the baby in the face!"* I ran over and got him out of the van. We sat down on the grass alongside the driveway and talked. "Why would you hit a little baby? - She is only *eight-months-old!*" I said. *"She hit me first!"* he said, in a very defensive tone. Knowing that wasn't true and needing to protect both babies, I called the social worker to see if maybe there was another foster home where Joaquin could be placed and would be the youngest, so he *wouldn't* pose a threat to anyone. She agreed that he should be moved, but asked if I could keep him over the weekend. That was no problem. Both Saturday and Sunday, I took some time to talk with him. For such a young boy, Joaquin was very articulate. When we discussed Kindergarten and how he liked going to school, I also asked him if he knew what he wanted to be when he grew up. "Yep!" he answered immediately. "I want to be just like my dad and join a gang and kill people."

"We must not, in trying to think
about how we can make a big difference,
ignore the small daily differences
we can make which, over time,
add up to big differences that
we often cannot foresee."
Marian Wright Edelman

WINTER

Yes, I had a reputation for taking the sicker babies and the more traumatized older kids, but this was over-the-top. Winter was a brown haired, bright blue-eyed 10-year-old girl, who almost always wore her hair in braids, loved lip-gloss and had a bunch of bracelets on both wrists. Tragically, one morning she found her birth mom dead from a drug overdose. The so-called problems of *my* life just disappeared after hearing about this. What could I say or do that would make it better? Love can make even the worst of circumstances seem bearable, and to quote Paul Tillich, "The first duty of love is to listen." so, I listened and I listened, and she poured out. This is what Winter said happened that morning. It was a school day, and her older brother routinely left for school way before she even got up. So, like always, Winter got up, got ready, and watched cartoons until it was time to leave for school. This particular day, she hadn't heard her mom up and it was getting late. She opened her mom's bedroom door and yelled, "*Mom!* We have to leave in 15 minutes - *Get up!*" She went back to watching television. After another 15 minutes, she realized that her mom hadn't gotten up. Not that unusual, she went in her mom's room and began to shake her. She was ice cold. Winter called 9-1-1, but it wasn't until the police and paramedics came, that she realized her mom was dead. Winter said she longed for a "normal" life, so living as part of our family day-to-day, with a consistent routine and minimal stress, was helpful to her, and made her content, but it was daily prayer that was critical in escaping the psychological torment she suffered from after the death of her mom, and in healing the emotional scars resulting from years of neglect and mistreatment from the time she was born. To pray with her at first, and to look into her sad eyes, or those of *any* foster child for that matter, or even to see the wasted life of a drug addict is to see the evidence of Satan's hold on this world. It lit a fire under me to come to God in my prayers with more boldness. During this time, my birth children were continuing to learn what sacrifice and service meant. To hear their prayers change from asking for "stuff," to giving thanks for everything, and *not* taking all that we were blessed with for granted, was music to my ears. Winter once told us that she would never forgive herself because just a week before her mom's death she was so sick of her, the drug use and lack of predictability, she told her mom she "hated" her. I couldn't wait to see how God would heal her. One Sunday afternoon she was thumbing through her bible and came across a scripture (Isaiah 30:18) that read, "So the Lord must wait for you to come to him so he can show you his love and compassion. For the Lord is a faithful God. Blessed are those who wait for his help." Through this specific scripture, Winter realized she was forgiven through God and that He had not forgotten her sadness and heartbreak. He had a unique plan for her life that included His love, compassion and healing.

"Blessed are those who mourn,
for they will be comforted."
Matthew 5:4

TUCKER
For the most part, Tucker was easy to take care of. A 23-month-old, tiny little toe-head blonde, he barely said a word, but charmed us all with his cleft chin and unbelievably adorable smile. The problem was, that anytime our family was returning home and approaching the front door, Tucker would freak out. He'd be happy the whole time we were out, and then, when we returned, it was as if you flipped a switch. Tucker would avoid getting close to the front door, and start to panic and cry. This went on every time we approached our front door for at least two months, and without any success, I tried several ways of getting him in the house without incident. One day, I brought it up to his social worker, asking

her if she knew why he might be reacting this way. "Well," she said, "I've got a pretty good idea. Mom got in trouble for repeatedly leaving Tucker in her car, strapped into his car seat, while she went into bars to party at night. After that, she admitted she never did *that* again, but instead would pick him up from daycare, go home, unlock the door of her apartment it, and shove him in. Then she would lock the door and leave Tucker alone, while she stayed out all night." H. Jackson Brown, Jr. said, "Love is when the other person's happiness is more important than your own." Children like Tucker, who have suffered torment such as this, even when removed from their abusive family environment, often have to endure quite an extensive journey to experience healing. Love and long-term stability is crucial, not only in breaking the cycle of abuse, but also in healing the emotional wounds resulting from years of mistreatment.

"I waited patiently for the Lord to help me,
and he turned to me and heard my cry."
Psalm 40:1 (NLT)

KELLY

For years, 11-year-old Kelly had to fend for herself while her drug-addicted mom sat around getting high on methamphetamines. Kelly was angry most of the time, and had a history of bad behaviors including aggression towards others. When we first met, her arms and legs were crossed, and she made no eye contact. Told she was disobedient, defiant, and even aggressive, she was to be watched very closely. When I talked with her about her behavior, she said, "I was only being bad so my mom would pay attention to *me* instead of her drugs." Not surprisingly, when children are first placed in a foster home, there is usually a period of time affectionately called the "honeymoon period," where the child behaves especially well. A good guess as to why is that they are scared and don't know what will happen if they break the rules, so they seem to be extra careful in the beginning, trying to be nearly perfect. Lots of children don't have a reference for simply being listened to, talked to, or lovingly being corrected when they make a mistake. Instead, they are pulling their head out of a wall, trying to figure out what they did wrong. If time is taken to point out nearly everything they do *right*, and they are praised for good behaviors, chances are those good behaviors continue, even after the honeymoon period has ended. This is because they get used to, and enjoy being treated well, and being given positive attention. Leo Buscaglia said, "Too often we underestimate the power of a touch, a smile, a kind word, a listening ear, an honest compliment, or the smallest act of caring, all of which have the potential to turn a life around." Unfortunately, there was no honeymoon phase for Kelly. She tested me quite a bit. She kept waiting to see if she would get yelled at or hit. Day after day, Kelly kept acting out. I would pray and pray for her, and hang in there with her, at the same time dissuading all the other children in the household from behaving like her. During past experiences, when I felt a little battle weary, God helped me to realize that victory is mine through Him. He is still on the throne and will save our children. We just need to have the courage to pray for them in boldness. Harold Hulbert said, "Children need love, especially when they do not deserve it." One day, Kelly finally understood that she was safe here and her attitude and behavior completely turned around. When I told her how well she was doing, and what a nice surprise it was, she began to cry and said in a sweet voice, " Everyone who ever loved me, hurt me. I have been waiting my whole life to be good for someone. You are just the first person that was ever really nice to me."

"God specializes in surprise endings."
Author Unknown

TOMMY

A long time child of neglect, I picked up Tommy in one of the worst conditions I had ever seen a child of his age. He was a 7-year-old second grader, filthier than you can imagine. He was wearing a men's shirt, that looked like it was recently pulled from a dumpster with grime around the neck and arm holes, filthy jeans that were torn and stained, and old worn shoes with almost no sole left. Tommy's hair hadn't been cut in a long time. It was past his shoulders, straight, dirty, and had lice. His fingernails were long and dirty, and he all he had with him was a smoky, torn back-pack with one of the straps fastened together with three large paperclips. He quietly got into my car and the fifteen-minute drive was almost more than I could handle. It was a warm late spring day, and the smell coming from his foot fungus was almost unbearable. First stop - Target for some shoes and clothes. I figured I would buy Tommy new shoes and discard his old ones right there at the store. I asked him to slip on the new ones to make sure they fit. When he took his foot out of the shoe, I saw that the bottom of his once white socks were *black*. "Wait!" I said. "Let's just compare the shoes side-by-side, then put them on at home after a nice, warm shower!" He agreed. After a haircut and new clothes, Tommy looked great going to school the next morning. With his beautiful brown Hispanic skin, he looked incredible in the powder blue collared shirt he wore, new jeans, and the white tennis shoes he picked out. When we arrived at his school, we walked past a teacher and about five students at the flagpole, getting ready to raise the flag. The teacher saw Tommy and gasped! She stopped what she was doing and hugged him. As her eyes welled up with tears, she quietly said, *"Thank you! Thank you!* You must be the foster parent!

I have *never* seen him look so good!" She continued to shake her head in amazement. "Thank you *so much*," she said again, quietly. "I had Tommy in my class last year and thought he had just slipped through the cracks." She hugged him one more time, then we said goodbye, and went on to his classroom. He was beaming as we walked in, and I introduced myself to his teacher. She had a similar reaction when she saw him appear from behind me. Many children were already in the classroom when we arrived. They all couldn't help but notice the changes in Tommy. When I was about to leave Tommy's classroom, his teacher said, "Oh! - You might want to stop by the principal's office on your way out, and tell her you have Tommy. She'll wonder why he didn't come to her office this morning." It turned out, this principal brought a clean washcloth to school every day, and personally washed Tommy's face and hands before school every morning. That is amazing love. Mahatma Gandhi said, and this principal exemplified it: "You must *be* the change you wish to see in the world."

> "If it is encouraging, let him encourage;
> if it is contributing to the needs of others,
> let him give generously;
> if it is leadership, let him govern diligently;
> if it is showing mercy, let him do it cheerfully."
> **Romans 12:8**

JACQUELINE

There was just too much noise coming from this little 4-year-old's room for her to be napping, so I peeked in on her. It was obvious she was just pretending to be asleep. I said in a low tone, "You had better be asleep!" She responded with a quiet confidence, "I am."

"When you can't sleep, don't count sheep.
Talk to the Shepherd."
Author Unknown

PARKER

One time, I loaded all the kids in the car to go give one of our birth moms a surprise visit with her cute little baby boy, Parker. Parker had fair skin and bright blue eyes, and unlike any baby I had ever had, he coo'd and ah-boo'd and goo'd for us almost on cue. Heather was baby Parker's birth mom, and she was really working her drug treatment program. It was clear that Heather's dad, Mike, a great guy, was supporting her 100%. It was nice to see this happening. Like I tell all my birth mom's, I won't work harder than *you* do, but if I see you really doing a great job, with permission, I will surprise you with extra visits, bring you pictures of your child, or show up at your program and give you a chance to show off your baby. So, it was now time to make good on my promise. We headed to Heather's program, and on the way, one of my other foster children, Kaelie, an 11-year-old girl, asked why we were surprising Heather. I told her that Heather was doing everything she was supposed to be doing in order to get Parker back. She was working her program, taking the parenting classes, staying in contact with her social worker, going to counseling, and probably the thing that impressed all of us most, was that she made no excuses about having messed up. After meeting up with Heather and giving her a nice little surprise visit with Parker, we were about to leave, when Kaelie leaned forward from the back seat of the van and asked if she could tell Heather something. I called Heather back over, hopped out and opened the side door of the van. Kaelie looked right at Heather and said to her, "I just wanted to tell you that I wish my mom was like you, and did what *she* was supposed to do, to get *me* back. I don't think most parents realize that all of us kids try to be patient and wait, but it is *so hard*. I am *really* proud of you. I wish I could give you a hug I am so proud of you!" With tears in her eyes, Heather leaned in, and let Kaelie give her a hug, and again Kaelie said, "I am proud of you." [Kaelie's birth mom never did do what she needed to do to get her back and her rights were terminated.] I wish every addict with kids in foster care could hear the words and wisdom coming from this child.

"Out of the mouth of babes!" (Paraphrased)
Matthew 21:16

"Now all glory to God, who is able, through his
mighty power at work within us,
to accomplish infinitely more than
we might ask or think."
Ephesians 3:20 (NLT)

DELLA & JOVITA

After being molested by their mom's live-in boyfriend, these sisters, Della and Jovita, ages 10 and 13, came to our home. They were very quiet, at least around *our* family. Maybe our difference in culture played a factor in that; they were Hispanic. They both spoke English well, but Spanish was their first language. As a family, we went the extra mile, literally, to keep them in the same schools they were attending before coming into the system. Della, the younger one, was finishing elementary school, and Jovita was finishing middle school, both landmark school years. Both girls had shoulder length, thick black hair that was so shiny it looked wet. They were overweight and often gazed downward, allowing their long bangs to cover their faces. They refused eye contact and made it difficult for any of us to get to know them. Preferring to stay in their room, getting them to come out, even for a meal, was arduous. It was strange, whenever we had dinner, neither Della nor Jovita would do much more than pick at their food, and shuffle it around their plates. Whatever I offered them, they declined. Maybe they ate at school? Then came the weekend. They still didn't eat much, and continued isolating themselves in their bedroom. After three weeks of this, I finally decided to check their room when they were at school one day. Boy, was I surprised! Della and Jovita had successfully foraged food and brought it into their room. In their dresser was everything from bags of chips, cookies, string cheese, a container of juice, a tall bottle of Pepsi, and hidden under their beds, was an amazing amount of trash. Everything from empty bread bags, juice containers, apple cores, banana peels, empty cereal boxes, an empty jello box, empty soda cans, empty water bottles, beef jerky wrappers, orange peel, and even some fast food trash. Some of it they took from our kitchen and pantry; some they had brought in. Even more shocking, I found the belt my 15-year-old son had been missing for two weeks, little toys and sweets from our 2-year-old's Easter basket, my 18-year-old daughter's new shirt that she already had spent hours looking for, some of my nice stationery, and something else out of nearly every room in the house. How devastating this was! Sitting at the foot of Jovita's bed, I prayed about what to do, and how to handle it. There was 3-1/2 hours before picking them up from school. I thought it would be best to take everything that didn't belong to them, and lay it neatly on their beds. When we returned home after school, I walked to their room with them, sat down on the window seat and said, "I need you girls to explain this." Expressionless, they both denied everything, and said that someone must have put all of it in their room. Feelings of sadness filled me. I thought about the abuse they suffered that brought them here. I learned that when someone has taken something from you as a little girl, you often steal things in an attempt to get back, that which was taken. The problem is that stealing things does *not* give back that which was stolen. Dear Heavenly Father, thank you for these two young girls, Della and Jovita. Bless them now and in the future with safety and love. Please allow complete healing and restoration in these girls as only You can do. I pray they will seek you, Lord. I pray they will find you, know you, press into you, and in their healing and restoration glorify You! Amen.

> "Someone may have stolen your dream
> when it was young and fresh
> and you were innocent.
> Anger is natural. Grief is appropriate.
> Healing is mandatory.
> Restoration is possible."
> **Jane Rubietta**

LUKE

It was day two, and we had just returned from shopping to get 11-year-old Luke some clothes. He was so excited to be able to pick out new things. More than anything, he couldn't believe he got ten pairs of the loose fitting, soft cotton boxer underwear. That afternoon, when I went in his room to make sure he had successfully hung up all his new clothes and his jacket, he said for the second time, "Thank you for the underwear." Answering mostly with my smile and eye contact, I quietly said, "Sure!" Then Luke looked at me with the most sincere smile and said, "I have never had underwear before."

> "Suppose a brother or sister is
> without clothes and daily food.
> If one of you says to him, 'Go, I wish you well;
> keep warm and well fed,'
> but does nothing about his physical needs, what
> good is it? In the same way,

faith by itself, if it is not accompanied by action,
is dead."
James 2:15-17

SHANNA SUE

Shanna Sue entered foster care because her mom went to jail for drugs. She was a beautiful 10-year-old girl with shiny light brown hair and an infectious laugh. We all got a kick of the silly things she did like fill her fortune cookie up with soy sauce before eating it, wear her hair in crazy hair styles, get everyone in the house hooked on passion tea, eat an entire plate of sliced bell pepper, wear necklaces on her head like a head band, and put lemon pepper on everything she ate. She got the all-time award for hitting the 'snooze' button on her alarm the most times in one morning while still managing to get out the door for school on time. Shanna Sue was pure energy, joy and laughter. One hot summer afternoon, we were all outside on the driveway washing the limo together. It had been decided that when we finished drying it off, we would all pile in, and cruise up and down Grand Avenue singing and having fun. When it was time to dry it off, she offered to go into the laundry room and get some more rags. She went running in, and then moments later came running out with blood dripping down her back, soaking her shirt. Shanna Sue had jumped up on the counter top to reach above the sink for the rags and hit her head on an open cupboard door. When she came outside she was screaming, "*Please* don't take me to the hospital, *please* don't take me to the hospital, *pllleeaassseeee*!!!" I took a closer look, and her head was split open and definitely in need of medical care. Just as a courtesy, I called Shanna Sue's birth mom to see if she would like to meet us at the hospital. Most birth parents, given the opportunity to show up for doctor visits, shots or even an emergency situation such as this one, surprisingly decline the offer. This mom and her boyfriend were waiting there when we pulled up. She lovingly held Shanna Sue on her lap for hours, while we waited for the staff to treat everything from an elderly patient with chest pain, to a guy with a kidney stone, to a man suffering from an industrial accident. It seemed like anyone who entered the ER, got to scoot past us in line. It had been several hours when Shanna Sue's mom handed her boyfriend money and asked him if he would go get some food. She graciously treated all of us to dinner. In addition to how well she did that evening, she worked her program, attended parenting classes and counseling, got a job and a place to live and reunified with her child. It was icing on the cake to be sitting on the beach with all the kids a few months later when she called from the courthouse to tell us the case was officially closed, and to express her sincere gratitude once more for caring for her daughter. It was a beautiful site to watch this birth mom step up to the plate and be the mom that God intended for her to be.

> "Treat people as if they were what they ought to be,
> and you help them to become
> what they are capable of being."
> **Johann Wolfgang von Goethe**

JARED

Jared, a little five-year-old African American boy, was energetic and funny, and had a huge, contagious smile with all his cute little white baby teeth. He and his four siblings were in the system because their mom and dad were in jail for drugs, and after going out to their house, the social worker said, "It was no place for a child to live." Cockroaches, trash and filth; there was little food, no beds, and drug paraphernalia was in plain sight. All five children were malnourished and it showed in Jared's weight and skin. Because it was so dry and flaky, his skin almost appeared white, especially on the arms, legs, feet and hands. About an hour-and-a-half after taking a bath the first evening, as instructed, Jared came downstairs and hopped up beside me on the couch. Grabbing the baby lotion, I swung his legs across my lap and asked permission to put some lotion on him. He smiled and said, "Sure! Why not!" I squirted a little in the palm of my hand and starting from his knee, smoothed it downward. His skin soaked it in so fast. His whitish skin turned a beautiful cocoa brown color instantly. That was when he screamed! "*Hey!* What choo doin' wit my skin, Miss Heidi?" He jerked his legs away. "I am using this lotion to make your skin like new again!" I answered. "Does that stuff have *brown* in it?" Jared asked. "Nope!" I said, as I just couldn't help but smile. It took a little explaining and some encouragement to continue, but he eventually let me continue. It wasn't long before he came to appreciate both "lotion time" and his natural, *beautiful* skin color.

"For you were made in my image."
Genesis 1:27 (Paraphrased)

DAISY

Daisy, a slender, sweet 9-year-old who had been physically abused, was an absolute delight, but her birth mom was especially difficult to deal with. Whenever she talked to Daisy, I was required to monitor the phone call, and would hear it all. I heard her ask some appropriate questions like, "How are you doing?" and "Did you have a good day at school?" and "What did you have for dinner?" but more often than not, she asked terribly inappropriate and offensive questions. One time, when she heard that we had chicken, sticky rice and broccoli for dinner, then watermelon for dessert, she asked in a derogatory tone, "Did Heidi give you *frozen* chicken??" Amazed, my initial reaction could have easily been to say, "*Yes!* - I gave her *frozen* chicken, but I don't have a live-in boyfriend that I let abuse her!" But this

wasn't about me, it was about the mother's actions and their
repercussions. I think had Daisy eaten even Mac n' Cheese
every night, it still would have been an improvement over
what she went through in her never-to-be-safe home. Daisy
would be fine here, but her brother kept being moved from
foster home to foster home because of their mom's actions.
How utterly selfish she was to offend the very people, volun-
teers, who were taking care of her children. After praying
and praying about how to better the situation, I gave Daisy's
birth Mom an invitation to join us at our home for dinner
one night. She accepted. After we all sat down at the dinner
table, Daisy excitedly asked if she could say the prayer. She
began by giving thanks for the food and especially for her
mom being able to come join us. At the end of the prayer, she
prayed, "...in the name of Jesus Christ, Amen." At that point,
her Mom looked up and sternly said to her, *"Next time you
pray in name of Buddha!"*

"Great is the Lord! He is most worthy of praise!
No one can measure his greatness.
Let each generation tell its children
of your mighty acts;
let them proclaim your power.
I will meditate on your majestic, glorious splendor
and your wonderful miracles.
Your awe-inspiring deeds will be on every tongue;
I will proclaim your greatness.
Everyone will share the story
of your wonderful goodness;
they will sing with joy about your righteousness.
The Lord is merciful and compassionate,
slow to get angry and filled with unfailing love.
The Lord is good to everyone.
He showers compassion on all his creation.
All of your works will thank you, Lord,

and your faithful followers will praise you.
They will speak of the glory of your kingdom;
they will give examples of your power.
They will tell about your mighty deeds
and about the majesty and glory of your reign.
For your kingdom is an everlasting kingdom.
You rule throughout all generations."
Psalm 145: 3-13 (NLT)

ADAM

Adam was born a drug-addicted baby, who was reunified with his parents at age one, only to live the next nine years of his life with his homeless drug-addicted parents, before he went back into foster care as a result of neglect. He came to us with long, dirty, lice-filled hair, scabies, and foot fungus. He was so dirty that I had no idea he had such fair skin until after he showered. Adam came across to us as defeated, lost, and lacking a sense of himself. By his frequent questions, you could tell that he perceived life as totally unpredictable. He had no goals, dreams or interests. For Adam, life was about survival. His big brown eyes and long eyelashes made you want to give him anything he asked for, and even though initially he had no manners, life skills, or common sense, you couldn't help but love this 10-year-old boy. Our family was used to frequent outings. During the first week Adam was with us, just merely talking about going somewhere seemed to create a lot of anxiety for him. He always assumed we would be leaving him at the house. "No. You're going *with* us." I would say as I watched Adam take a deep breath. It didn't begin to make sense until our first trip to the mall. We were not even inside yet, when he pointed to someone and said, "My babysitter! - Can I go say hi?" We all hurried to catch up with her, and introduced ourselves. She didn't look especially happy to see him, but smiled and said a quick "hi" then walked away. *Huh!* I thought. Then, less than an hour later, Adam saw someone else he knew - *another* babysitter! This was a young man who was somewhat friendlier, but didn't know Adam's name until he was reminded. Two days later, we attended the grand opening of the new skate park in town, where Adam saw *two more* of his babysitters! It didn't take long to realize that his parents left him with pretty much anyone that would watch him. After some time, he began to share many of his scary experiences with us, and when we asked him how he got through it, you could see the mental struggle in his face as he begrudgingly answered, "I secretly prayed." All of us were curious, and asked Adam to tell us more. He continued, "Well, one night, when my dad took me to have dinner at a church that feeds the homeless, some man sitting next to me whispered in my ear, 'God hears and answers your prayers.' So, even though I didn't know if it was true or not, I kept praying *every night* that I would have a normal life like other kids." We were all so touched by Adam's story. My prayer is that kid's like Adam who pray, and have yet to have their prayers answered, never think that God's *delays* are God's *denials*.

> "Courage doesn't always roar.
> Sometimes courage is the quiet voice
> at the end of the day saying,
> 'I will try again tomorrow.'"
> **Mary Anne Radmacher**

ELIZABETH

Elizabeth's mom called 9-1-1, and after describing the symptoms to the nurse, was told that her four-month-old baby was probably having a seizure. They explained to the mom that she needed to bring her baby into the ER *immediately*. Eleven hours later, mom came in with Elizabeth. Because of her delay, it was deemed 'medical neglect,' and the hospital put a hold on the baby. The courts agreed, and

Elizabeth went into foster care. When I came for her, I could hear her screaming from down the hall. Elizabeth was very irritable and appeared noticeably scared by the way her eyes were open so wide. The nurses were very caring, but had given up on trying to soothe her. I picked Elizabeth up and held her close, humming quietly. I felt her take a couple deep breaths and calm down a bit. Moving slowly, I put her in the car seat and headed home. The next several days were tough. She needed a terrible tasting medicine for seizures that had to be given orally, and the i.v. area was still sore. Her skin had rashes and bumps everywhere. On day four, I was well on my way to getting to know her. Her skin was starting to clear up. We figured out how to best give her the medicine and she seemed calmer. It hadn't even been a week later, and the birth mom had her first visit with Elizabeth. One of the questions she asked me with all seriousness was, "Would you like to know some things that my baby likes?" "Of course!" I said, thinking she might let me know Elizabeth's favorite position for sleeping, or how to get a good burp out of her, or ways she liked to be soothed. I was wrong. "Well, she likes French onion dip, strawberries, Pepsi and Dr. Pepper, hmmm, what else.... ummm.... Oh! -*OH*! - dill pickles - you just put 'em in her mouth and she sucks on them!" she said. We have all seen and heard things that are shocking, and this definitely qualified. Elizabeth's birth mom did not end up getting her baby back, but a very loving couple, who had been trying to have a baby for many years, was blessed with her, and she with them, as her "forever family."

"I pray that your love will overflow more and more,
and that you will keep on growing in knowledge
and understanding."
Philippians 1:9 (NLT)

CODY

A very quiet 7-year-old, Cody was tall and mature for his age, had fair skin, brown hair, brown eyes and very long eyelashes that made you jealous. He came to us right from the hospital with second and third degree burns down the side of his face, neck and chest. His dad was at the stove, boiling water when his mom called from Iraq. Mom gave Dad the bad news that she wouldn't return for another three months, which upset him so badly that he splashed the boiling water on Cody. I spent the next two days telling Cody he wasn't for hurting, and reassuring him that his dad would be given help in dealing with his anger problem, and support in handling his feelings so that hopefully something like this would never happen again. We prayed together for his complete healing and for patience in getting through this. On the third day, they placed Cody back with his dad. It was interesting because it made me realize that when God turns things around from bad to good, it seems easy to understand; but when difficult situations remain difficult, or I am not happy about a particular outcome, or there is something terrible or unexpected that has happened, I don't always fully understand God. What I know without any uncertainty is that although I may sometimes get caught up in what may be *temporarily* good, God is interested in what is *eternally* good. He can see around corners. Dear God, Thank you for your infinite wisdom. Thank you that you are God and I am not. Please bless Cody today and all the days of his life that he might be safe and protected from all harm, and be able to grow up knowing you, loving you, wanting to serve you and be like you, and in all that he is and does, glorify You! Amen.

"Be strong and of good courage,
do not fear nor be afraid of them;
for the Lord your God, He *is* the One
who goes with you.

He will not leave you nor forsake you."
Deuteronomy 31:6 (NKJV)

JULIA

Julia, a 7-year-old in second grade, was the neglected daughter of a meth addict, who was thrown in jail following a drug bust. Julia was a very thin, fair-skinned girl with stringy, long strawberry-blonde hair. With big green eyes, and freckles across her cheeks, she was very cute, but said to have *not* been at all cooperative with the social worker during the initial interview. "She is totally protecting her mother and her mother's boyfriend," the social worker mentioned in frustration. Julia was afraid and had a very low self-esteem. She didn't want much for herself. A couple days after she settled in our home, we were sitting together on the floor, cutting out fabric to make her a small purse. The look on her face said she had a lot on her mind when she asked, "Can I sit on your lap?" She then quickly retracted her question by saying, "I change my mind." "What's up?" I asked her. "I am afraid," Julia said, as she was cutting out what would later become the handle of the purse. "My social worker told me to tell the truth and I *want* to, but I am afraid I will never get to see my mommy again if I do." "Well..." I explained. "Whatever you tell the social worker, they can help your mom with. Let's say you told that she had a problem with alcohol. Then, they would give her an alcohol class. And if you said she had an anger problem, they would give her an anger management class. And if you said she yells at you, and isn't too nice of a mommy, they would give her a parenting class. Whatever you say she has a problem with, they will give her a class for that - It's actually pretty neat. You can help her in a way." Julia still looked very unsettled. "Do you want to pray and ask God if He can help you be a truthful girl?" I asked. "Okay." she answered. Closing my eyes, I bowed my head to pray. I took a deep breath and silently asked God for the words to say, when to my surprise, *she* started praying! Julia gave thanks for many things and prayed that God would help her to tell the truth. The way she prayed so sweetly made my eyes well up with tears. When she finished, she asked if she could have a hug, then jumped on my lap. From there, she started sharing all about these "little pieces of foil in mommy's closet that smelled really weird." She said her mommy and the boyfriend would go in their room for hours and hours at a time, leaving her and her 4-month-old baby brother in the living room alone. She would smell a weird smell and sometimes she heard her mommy and mommy's boyfriend yelling at each other. Julia said, when her baby brother would cry, her mommy would yell through the door for her to feed him or pick him up, but she didn't know how to make a bottle and the baby was too heavy for her to pick up. Julia sobbed when she admitted that she accidentally dropped him once and even though he was screaming, her mom didn't come out of her room to help. She said how scared she was, that she might drop him again. She also shared that she loved to go to school and said it was one of the only places she ever felt happy. After getting her social worker on the phone, Julia agreed to repeat everything. In the six months she stayed with us, Julia sat on my lap being held, many, many times. She gained a positive self-image, taught all of us how to pray like a child, showed us a thing or two about being truthful, and brought to mind in a very meaningful way that a child is never too old to be held in a mothers arms.

> "The truth, which has made us free,
> will in the end, make us glad also."
> **Felix Adler**

CONNOR

The court was getting ready to send Connor, a 10-year-old child, and his 7-year-old sister Samantha, back to their parents. They came into the system three years earlier, very underweight and having been beaten by their parents. Just before a child's return, it is not uncommon for them to be interviewed by an investigator from the Public Defender's office. When Connor was asked if he had any concerns about returning to his mother, he answered, "Only two - that I won't get enough food and that she'll hit me every day." It was about 5 months after he was reunified, when I received a phone call from him. I heard his sister crying in the background, and Connor was asking if he could come back to live with us. Knowing there was a conflict, I offered to talk with his mom. "She's gone for the weekend," he said. "Okay, then, how can I help you solve the problem you are having?" I asked. Still crying, he answered, "My mom left us $2 to go to the store and get dinner, and before I got a chance to choose anything, Samantha spent the whole thing on a Coke and Lucas lollipops!" There was not a lot that could be done in this particular instance besides listen and be supportive, because the child now lived an hour away. But after thinking about all the times I have seen unkempt children all alone in stores pulling coins out of their pockets to buy candy, there now was a new perspective on it. With this awareness, my feelings of reluctance that kept me from handing them money, were now changing. Dear God, please give me discernment; open my eyes, and bring my attention to any child who is truly in *need*, that I might be able to respond. Holy Spirit, encourage me to become an agent of change. Amen.

"You must each decide in your heart
how much to give.
And don't give reluctantly or
in response to pressure.

91

For God loves a person who gives cheerfully."
2 Corinthians 9:7 (NLT)

KIMBER & ARIANNA

Early one winter, I got two little girls, Kimber and Arianna, both with fair skin, black shiny hair and big green eyes surrounded by long, dark eyelashes. They were ages 6 and 8-years-old, and were in the car with their dad when he got arrested for driving under the influence. They screamed helplessly as he was handcuffed and taken away to jail, right in front of them. On the third day in our home, we were in the living room, enjoying a fire in the fireplace talking, when Kimber said, "You know what? I am *relieved* that this happened. You wanna know why?? I am sleeping *so much better* now!" Surprised, I asked her why. "Well, at my school, they told us people can *die* from alcohol, and since I know my dad drinks alcohol in the garage at night time, I hide under the kitchen table where I can see if he comes out of his bedroom to go to the garage and drink. I stay up because I want to know if he is going to be okay. I know my step mom quit drinking because I hear her telling dad to please stop." "Did *you* ever ask him not to drink anymore?" I asked. "Yeah, but he thinks Arianna and I are stupid." "Why would he think that?" I asked. "Because he tells us all the time that he doesn't drink anymore. He thinks we don't know what he's doing when he goes in the garage and makes us stay out, or locks himself in the bathroom. He also leaves us in the car when he goes into the liquor store. He says she is just buying cigarettes, but he comes out with a bag. I wish I wasn't too scared to tell him that he isn't fooling anyone."

"And you will know the truth,
and the truth will set you free."
John 8:32 (NLT)

92

RILEY

This little 9-month-old baby was so insecure. Whenever I so much as turned my back, even to answer the phone, he would scream, not cry, but *scream*! I knew he would be a handful, since the previous foster mom lasted only *two days* before putting in her 7-day notice that she (sadly) needed to have him moved. She complained that she could not get anything done! Wanting more information, and hoping to understand what Riley went through more fully, I talked to the social worker. I learned that his mom was a 25-year-old drug addict who worked the streets as a prostitute. One day, the mom asked a 19-year-old girl, who lived in her low-income housing project, if she could watch Riley, just for a couple of hours. Mom handed the baby off so quickly, she didn't really give the teen a chance to say no. Five hours later, it was time for the teen to go to work, and still the mom hadn't come back for Riley. The 19-year-old didn't even know Riley's mother's name or where she lived, so she gave Riley to someone else. He was handed off several times before the police were called. Making perfect sense, Riley became insecure and fearful. Life taught him that when someone leaves, they might not come back. After much prayer about how to make him feel secure, I dragged out of my baby things a soft cotton baby sling and carried him around in it for about two weeks, only taking it off when I held him to feed him, or when it was time to lie him down in his crib. Even then, ocean sounds were religiously played as something consistent for him to hear as he fell asleep. In no time at all, he became content and secure. In spite of obstacles and discouragements he earned the title, "Happiest Baby Ever!" and with 80 or so competitors over the years, that was an amazing achievement!

"Where there is great love,
there are always miracles."
Willa Cather

93

RENÉE

Before being brought into the system, Renée, a very sweet little 6-year-old girl, was living at her grandparents house and sharing a room with her mom and a younger sibling. Mom was using methamphetamines daily. Renée was fearful and witnessed the drug use and heard lots of fighting between her mom and grandfather, until one day, her birth mom tried to kill her grandfather by stabbing him multiple times. When I went to pick up Renée, she ran right to me with her shiny long hair and eyes so dark they looked black. She had especially good posture and smiled an unforgettable smile with several teeth missing. Without any fuss, Renée got into my car. The drive home is different for every child. Many kids stay quiet, looking around. Some are chatty and offer up lots of information. Some just sit quietly, looking very pale. Some demand I put on *their* music. Some ask endless questions to find out what things are like and where we are going. Some dissociate and stare out the window. Some sleep. Some look at me but won't say a word. Some children are hyper and happy. Some are weepy and upset. Some tell me they are relieved that this happened. Some cry *for* their parents; more cry *because* of their parents. Within 10 minutes, Renée politely asked if she could unbuckle. "Why?" I asked. "So I can throw up out the window!" she answered. Renée coped with all that was going on by trying to please others, having a positive attitude, expressing herself through art, keeping her room neat and organized, offering to help, and doing well in school. She was constantly writing notes expressing her appreciation for all she had. She, at age six, was truly an inspiration. Richard Wagner said, "Joy is not in things; it is in us."

"I pray that God, the source of hope,
will fill you completely with joy and peace
because you trust in Him.

Then you will overflow with confident hope
through the power of the Holy Spirit."
Romans 15:13 (NLT)

ZACK

Zack, a 14-year-old boy who was a popular and well-liked straight 'A' student, entered the system after his mom's boyfriend was caught molesting his 11-year-old sister. It was a long and emotional first day, and he had finally decided to lie down on his bed at 10:10PM. About an hour later, and ready for bed myself, I first checked on the other children and then saw some light from under Zack's door. Quietly knocking, I asked through the door if I could come in. "Sure." I heard. "How are you doing, Zack?" I asked. "I'm okay," he answered. "Thanks for letting me come here," he continued. I told him I was sorry about the circumstances, but *glad* he was here. "Are you going to sleep soon?" I asked. "Yeah, you can turn off the light." "Did you already brush your teeth?" the Mom in me asked. "Oops!" Zack answered, as he simultaneously got up and headed into the bathroom. He brushed his teeth and returned to bed. "Sweet dreams!" I said while giving him a gentle pat on the forearm. "You, too." he said, looking exhausted. With a smile I said good night, stepped out of the room and turned the doorknob to quietly close the door. I heard a tired voice ask, "Do you think I can call my sister tomorrow?" Opening the door again, I answered, "Sure, I think we can make that work." He thanked me, and when closing the door I caught a glimpse of his eyes, welled up with tears. I silently prayed on his behalf, "Dear God, Thank you for this day. Thank you for bringing this new foster child into our home. Please allow him to feel welcomed and loved. Please bless Zack and his sister. Quell their fears, Lord, and show yourself to them. When they are sad, comfort them. Carry them through these difficult times with your amazing love. Give them the courage to trust You, and press into You.

Surround them and protect them with your heavenly angels as they sleep tonight. In Jesus' precious name, Amen."

> "Casting the whole of your care
> [all your anxieties, all your worries, all your
> concerns, once and for all]
> on Him, for He cares for you affectionately and
> cares about you watchfully."
> **1 Peter 5:7** (AMP)

MOLLY & MORGAN

Molly and Morgan were 9-year-old twin girls, living with their paternal grandfather because their Mom and Dad were both drug addicts, in and out of jail. Even though they were twins, their looks and personality couldn't have been any different. Molly was quite a bit taller, average size, with olive skin, light brown hair and green eyes. She was outgoing and talkative. Morgan was short and small framed, had much darker skin, dark brown hair and brown eyes. She tended to stay in the background and was more introverted. During the first month or so, they were a handful with their constant bickering and the endless battles to get them to clean their room, but like most children, they calmed down and before you knew it, acted very loving toward each other and found a special place in my heart. They had been with us for eight months or so, when it came time to be adopted by their maternal grandparents. Before they left, I asked, in an effort to improve things, "What were the best things and the worst things about living here?" Molly quickly answered, "Well, the *best* thing was earning Beanie Babies and glow-in-the-dark stars for good behavior!" Her twin agreed. "How about the worst thing?" Neither answered. *"Come on!"* I pleaded with a smile. After hemming and hawing for a good long time, and lots of back and forth, *"You* tell *her!"* "No! *You* tell *her*!!" *"NO! YOU tell her!"* Finally it came out. "Well,"

Morgan said, "The worst thing about living here was that you never offered us *coffee* in the morning!" I was shocked. They were only nine! "You girls drink *coffee*?" I asked. After a brief interrogation, they fessed up to what had gone on for the past three years, since they were six. It turned out that every morning, their grandfather would wake up at the crack of dawn to his automatic coffee maker having already brewed a pot for him. He would grab a cup and leave for work, long before the girls were awake. Each school day Molly and Morgan woke up, got dressed and walked to school on their own. But just prior to leaving the house, they would sit down and *finish* Grandpa's pot of coffee, and rinse the carafe out. No wonder they missed their coffee in the morning! As the years of providing foster care continued, I never did serve coffee to children in the morning, nor was I so naive as to think that Molly and Morgan were the only kids used to drinking it!

> "Pretty much all the honest truth telling there is in
> the world is done by children."
> **Oliver Wendell Holmes**

ANTHONY

Anthony, a little 6-year-old guy was hyper and fun and always made me laugh. While I drove, he loved singing *Unbreak My Heart* to everyone in the car, and no matter where we were, he would do cartwheels and other tricks to make us smile. He came into the system because his parents got busted for drugs, and his father, two uncles and nearly every other male in his family was incarcerated for charges related to domestic violence. When I first introduced him to God, I told him how He loves children very much and wants to hear their prayer requests. Anthony was surprised. "Really??" he asked. "Yup!" I answered. I could tell it provoked thought. Each night I asked him if he had a prayer request. On the third night, he finally shared his first request. With a serious look on his face, Anthony asked, "Can you pray that my Daddy don't kill my Mommy?"

"We must accept finite disappointment,
but we must never lose infinite hope."
Martin Luther King, Jr.

"God is our refuge and strength,
always ready to help in times of trouble."
Psalm 46:1 (NLT)

AUDREY

The social worker came to my home to visit Audrey, a new 11-year-old black girl I had just gotten. I had never taken an African American foster child before. I am white and my social worker was black. We were talking with this little girl, who had been through a terrible situation involving domestic violence, when she changed the subject abruptly and shared how excited she was about her hair! Having just braided it the day before, I said, "It actually turned out pretty good, considering I had never before worked with an African American's hair!" The reaction wasn't quite what I expected. The social worker said, "As far as I know, she's not from *Africa*!" Stunned, I replied, "Oh... sorry.... a *black* girl..." Then she said, "She doesn't look *black* to me; she looks *brown*." I was speechless. When the social worker left my home, I asked Audrey, "Were you offended or upset that I referred to you as an 'African American' girl?" "No," she answered, "but I was embarrassed at how my social worker made you feel bad." Audrey continued, "To me, all that doesn't matter. I think it's mostly about love." What wisdom! Audrey and I hugged, and then she skipped off to play, while I silently said a little prayer for the social worker. In my heart, I truly wish there were more "brown" people that volunteered to become foster parents.

> "If we pray, we will believe;
> if we believe, we will love;
> if we love, we will serve."
> **Mother Teresa**

SAM

Sam was a cute, red-headed boy with green eyes and freckles and was only 9-years-old when he became a foster child. His meth-addicted mom left him, his two brothers and sister, alone for over a week. The children's ages were 11, 9, 5 and 3. They were said to be living in filth amongst rodents and animal feces. Sam, who was the 9-year-old, could easily give a list of the only "foods" they had to eat: powdered coffee creamer, ketchup and mustard packets, hot sauce, spices, bacon bits, grape jelly and Italian dressing. They found a way to survive. His teacher for the entire previous year, and the first few weeks of the current year, said when he still didn't show up with a backpack the second week of school, she finally provided him with one herself. She said Sam arrived at school dirty, often wearing the same clothes for several days in a row. Around the middle of September, the first flyer for Party City came out, showcasing all the Halloween costumes. One day after school, while Sam sat eating his snack, I put the flyer in front of him and told him to read through it and decide which costume he would like. As he looked through the pages, I asked what he was last year. He hesitated, and then answered, "My sister dressed me up as a girl and the school sent me home." He laughed an embarrassed laugh. "Okay, well, *this* year, you are going to have a real costume!" I said, "and we are going to go get one the day they come out, so you get first pick." We did exactly that, and he picked out the Ninja fighter with all the accessory knives and swords. When we got home he wanted to try it on. "Of course!" I said. Then Sam asked if he could wear it while jumping on the trampoline. "I guess." I answered. The next day Sam asked if he could wear it when we went to the grocery store. "I don't see why not." I replied. A few days later he wanted to know if he could wear it to Costco. "Sure," I said. Sam must have worn it twenty or more times in the month before Halloween, and many, many times after Halloween was over. It was clear that this 9-year-old has missed out on the "dress up" time that most of our boys get where they are 3 and 4 and 5-years-old, when they run around in capes and play and imagine and dream. This experience allowed Sam to make up for that!

> "This is the day the Lord has made;
> let us rejoice and be glad in it."
> **Psalm 118:24**

JACI

Jaci was a 10-1/2-year-old girl, who was extremely skinny. Her eye color was so dark, it looked black, and she wore her hair pulled back in a tight ponytail. Jaci and her two younger sisters came into the system because her mom and mom's live-in boyfriend was beating them. Afraid to tell anyone, Jaci kept it to herself for a long time. The stress proved to be too much and she developed anxiety and anorexia by age 10. When I got her, she rarely made eye contact, didn't speak unless you asked her to, and would not ever come to the dinner table for a meal, unless she was told to. She was scared. I remember on the second night, just before bed, Jaci kept asking what the social worker was going to do, and if the judge said she could go back to her mom, and if her attorney was going to come talk to her again. "Those aren't things I know." I said. "I am just in charge of taking good care of you." I added. Then, I asked if she wanted to pray with

me. "I want to pray, but I don't know how. I'm Buddhist."
Jaci said, "I don't really know a lot about it, because we
never went to temple." It was amazing sharing with her that
there is a God bigger than any social worker, investigator,
or judge, who loves her and wants to hear and answer her
prayers. You could almost see the sense of hope that arose in
her. After church the next day, the whole family sat together
eating lunch. Jaci asked a number of questions about Christ,
then said with the innocence only a child has, "This man you
are talking about, Jesus Christ, I think I like him!" Awww,
I think I like Him, too! I thought. During the two years Jaci
was with us, our family was blessed by being able to witness
her beautiful journey, from her innocent questions arising
out of curiosity, to reading the Bible and getting to know
God, to watching her make Him the center of her life, and
accepting Him into her heart as her personal Savior! Wow! I
remember a time when Jaci was crying and crying because it
seemed to her that God had not answered her many prayers
to be reunified with her birth mom. I was comforting her and
trying to explain God's sovereignty by telling her that God
might say "no" to what you've asked Him for, because He
wants to give you something much better. A way to show
God that you will trust Him is to renew your commitment
to seek and follow His will, and don't forget those powerful
words that Christ himself uttered, "Ask and it will be given
to you; seek and you will find; knock and the door will be
opened to you." (Matthew 7:7)

"For I know the plans I have for you,"
declares the Lord,
"plans to prosper you and not to harm you,
plans to give you hope and a future."
Jeremiah 29:11

ROBERT

This 8-1/2-year-old chunky blonde-haired boy showed up with two big duffle bags loaded with every "thing" a child could ever want. Robert had the newest Playstation game-system and tons of games, a new CD player and all the most popular cd's, movies, electronic toys, expensive famous label clothing and shoes, and an attitude of entitlement that went along with it. Not impressed, it wasn't a surprise though, that all the children in my home, including my own kids, were. The birth parents had been thrown in jail after a drug bust, and Robert and his two siblings went to three different foster homes. There was nothing their parents could do from jail to make it better. They barked demands to the social worker to get all three kids in one home, but there just wasn't a foster home with three openings. After a few weeks, Robert was included on our family chore list. He was shocked he was expected to lift a finger! He also learned very quickly that there was no short order cook available in the kitchen, either. He was even used to bossing his teachers around and getting his way at school. Robert had been with us for about four and a half weeks and was still experiencing nightmares about the drug bust and how scary it was when it all went down. It was hard to comfort him because those nightmares weren't about monsters or things that didn't exist - it was his real life! Robert needed daily reassurance that he would be taken care of. He opened up on many occasions and took advantage of every bit of quality time, hugs, love and affection offered. When asked whether he got any quality time or affection Robert said that his parents were, ".... just not like that" and he never got anything but *stuff*. One night at the dinner table, Robert broke down, then had an epiphany and realized the fullness of our saying, "Stuff is not love." Although I have caused my own children to sacrifice and sometimes do without the "luxuries" their friends enjoy, there is no regret or unhappiness about any of my choices.

I am content in our family's service to God. It is a privilege to do without for His sake. The tragedy behind all of this for Robert was that just at the point in time when he was feeling especially loved in ways that had nothing to do with material items, his parents got him back, apologized to him for having to be in foster care, and "made it up to him" by lavishing he and his siblings with more *things*. Not quite a month after being returned to his parents, and just after dinner one night, the phone rang and it was Robert. It was a blessing to hear from him. We put him on speakerphone and when he heard all of us saying hi, he said, "Awwww, I miss *all* you guys and all the talks at the dining room table. That was so fun!" After everyone got a chance to talk with him, we eventually hung up the phone and I thought about that saying from Harold S. Hubert, "The greatest classrooms of this nation or any nation are not in any school or university. They're around the dinner tables in the homes." We later prayed for Robert's parents that they would understand how essential unconditional love is to their children's well being, and that no amount of *stuff* makes a child feel loved and wanted. We gave thanks for Robert having been here, getting to reunify with his parents, and prayed that they would continually assure their children, including Robert, that they would always be there for them no matter what.

(Speaking about love~)
"If you have it, you don't need anything else,
and if you don't have it,
it doesn't much matter what else you have."
James M. Barrie

LISA
Fair skin, green eyes and black shoulder length hair, the medical records indicated that this little 5-year-old girl had been sexually abused since before she had her first birthday.

I bought her all new clothes pretty much, and new shoes, socks and underwear - the kind that had the days of the week on them, since she was just learning to say the days in order. Each night, I offered to help her set her clothes out for the next day and she would never let me put her underwear out. Within the first week I figured out why. She liked to wear all of her panties at the same time; each and every clean pair she had, she wore. When I realized that she was doing this every day, I asked her why. She shrugged her shoulders and said, "I feel more safer."

> "Don't let your hearts be troubled.
> Trust in God, and trust also in me."
> **John 14:1** (NLT)

GREGORY

This little boy was just 2-1/2-years-old and had been physically abused. He was small for his age and had very fine blonde hair, like that of a baby. He didn't speak much, but communicated with us by grunting and pointing. When we brought him home, he was dirty, and smelled like cigarette smoke. A nice, warm bubble bath was prepared and I began to strip off his clothing. When I lifted Gregory's shirt, I saw bruises and little welts across his back. It made me so sad. Later that night, when I was praying for him and his healing, I couldn't help but compare what he had been through in his little life with what seemed like my minor troubles. I began to repent because I felt in my heart I was whining about seemingly unimportant, "little" things. Especially after seeing with my own eyes what Gregory had been through, my problems and complaints seemed so insignificant. I had just asked for God for forgiveness, when I heard a tiny knock at my bedroom door. When I opened it, there stood another foster child, an 11-year-old girl with tears in her eyes, holding her long slender finger out, saying she had just gotten a paper cut. Without any hesitation, I got the ointment and a Band-Aid and took care of her. She thanked me, then turned to walk down the hallway. She added a quiet, "I appreciate you," then went into her bedroom. After returning to prayer, I realized through her, that God *does* care about the "little" things - and that even a tiny paper cut is not petty or unimportant to God. Pouring from my heart, I prayed, Thank you, Lord that when we reach out to the broken hearted to love them, we learn from them as well. Help me to soothe when there is pain, reassure when a situation seems unbearable, give hope in times of grief, and to give my love unconditionally. Help me to remind the broken that they are still whole in Your sight. In Jesus' name, Amen.

"Blessed are those who trust in the Lord
and have made the Lord their hope and confidence."
Jeremiah 17:7 (NLT)

MARY

Mary was a very talkative 8-year-old girl, who came into the system when the school noticed that she and her 10-year-old sister had more than two weeks of unexcused absences. She had very pretty dark skin and light brown wavy hair. Her sister looked similar, was not much taller and was very underweight. Mary and her sister asked a zillion questions, but were most concerned when asking if I drink alcohol or take drugs. "Nope!" I answered. "Why not?" she asked. "Because I like to be extra responsible, so I can take good care of you!" I answered. "That's good," Mary replied. "I can see why at school they teach us not to drink alcohol or take drugs. My Mom does it a lot. Sometimes we walk to her friend's house down the street. They have a TV outside. The grown up's stay inside and smoke pot and drink alcohol. Once, we saw them blow smoke into their dog's face and everyone laughed. One night, my mom was walking so wobbly when we left to come home that her friend's husband had to walk with us to help my mom. Even though he was holding on to her, she still fell down," Mary said. "I am so sorry. What did you girls do?" I asked. "That night I cried really hard and told her to stop drinking. She got so mad at me she hit me on my back with a spatula. The next day when I told her that my back hurt, she said she never hit me. I think alcohol makes people lie."

> "We know the truth, not only by the reason,
> but also by the heart."
> **Blaise Pascal**

TYRÓN

Tyrón, a little 18-month-old with soft, wispy light brown hair, and coffee-with-too-much-cream skin, slept in one of the rooms opposite the wall of my bedroom. He had been abandoned at an early age, and was very timid, cowering like an abused animal whenever he made even a tiny mistake, like accidentally knocking over his sippy cup. Tyrón showed up at my house with a diaper rash that extended up to his belly button and a number of bruises. I don't understand how he could have been so neglected; he was the most loveable little guy you could ever imagine. Often in the early morning, I would hear something tapping against the wall. By the time I got out of bed and walked into the room he shared with his brother, it appeared that both kids were still asleep. One day, I asked his brother, a tough little 6-year-old, "What is up with the tapping?" "Oh, Miss Heidi, that's Tyrón's head against the wall. He does that if he wakes up wet." he answered. "Why?" I asked. "Because money don't grow on trees, and diapers are expensive. When he wets, he gets beat. That's the only way he's gonna learn!" Dear God, later this morning, I will be talking to Tyrón about tapping his head on the wall. He is frightened, Lord. Please give me the gentleness and warmth to comfort him, and through my eyes and smile and hugs may he know I care. Give me the kind of love and compassion that will calm his fears. In Jesus' name I pray, Amen.

> "He heals the brokenhearted
> and bandages their wounds."
> **Psalm 147:3** (NLT)

CHRISTY

Christy was barely 5-years-old, but really tall for her age. Her birth mom had physically abused her and her two brothers, and all three had been together in a different foster home until their mom tried to run over the previous foster parent with her car, in a parking lot after their visit. Mom undoubtedly had some anger issues that affected the behaviors of all three children. Christy was the middle child, and had soft skin, big brown eyes, light brown silky hair and dimples. The first two weeks with her was a dream. Perfect in every way, she tried so hard to please everyone around her. Overhearing me mention the baby was hungry, she offered, "I can make her a bottle! You put 2oz of water for one scoop of powder!" she said. Amazing, I thought. "Well, *I* will be the Mommy, and *you* can be the kid! - How does that sound?" I asked her. "Okay, I guess." she answered. In those first couple of weeks, Christy was just trying to figure out whether she was safe, because once she realized I wasn't going to hit or hurt her, or even raise my voice, she started acting out. One day, all of the kids and I left the grocery store after getting a special "fieldtrip" lunch for another child in our home. I was pushing the cart and Christy was standing right next to it. I noticed the very first car in the row leaving, and while pointing to it, said to everyone, "Let's wait and let her pull out." Immediately, Christy smiled, looked right into my eyes, then ran and dove behind the ladies car. All at once, I screamed for Christy, pulled the shopping cart backward and behind me, and dove forward for her. Thankfully, the lady heard the scream and stopped. Out of breath and shocked, I asked Christy, *"Why would you do that?? Why???"* Breathing quickly herself, Christy answered with a half smile, "Because I wanted her to hit me; I wanted to see what it would be like to be dead."

> "We are pressed on every side by troubles,
> but we are not crushed.
> We are perplexed, but not driven to despair.
> We are hunted down, but never abandoned by God.
> We get knocked down, but we are not destroyed."
> **2 Corinthians 4:8-9** (NLT)

JOSHUA

Joshua was a short, and very small-framed 10-year-old boy. He became a foster child after his birth mom was arrested for drugs and thrown into jail. The day I picked him up, he had shoulder length, dirty hair and was wearing a mens medium t-shirt and jeans that were 3 inches too short. He had a filthy, torn 'Bob the Builder' backpack, which reeked like cigarette smoke, and that he claimed to have had since Kindergarten. Joshua was in fourth grade, functioning at the first grade level. He was in special education and had an IEP (Individualized Education Program). He had previously gotten into fights and scuffles with other students, and in the last year, started skipping school all together. He said it was because he got tired of being bullied and made fun of. Needless to say, school was *not* something he looked forward to, like most kids his age. It's always a concern when the child isn't learning, but with Joshua, an equal concern was that he simply wasn't having a positive educational experience. Thinking it might lessen the teasing and bullying and even might make Joshua want to be at school, I helped out in his classroom, and volunteered to drive on fieldtrips. Not surprisingly, there is never a shortage of children that want to ride with you on a fieldtrip when your "car" is a limo. That was the case one late spring day when we volunteered and took it with Joshua's 4th grade classroom to the Wild Animal Park. At the end of the day, but before returning to the school, all the kids, parents and teachers reconvened in the parking lot. The kids that *didn't* ride with us, wanted to get in, and with permission from the teachers, each child got a spin around the parking lot. Joshua got to pick which kids took a turn riding in the limo next, and he rode with each group, as we circled round and round the large parking lot. Joshua "showed off" turning on and off the twinkle lights and putting the privacy glass up and down. Finally it was time to return our group of children back to the school and go home. The whole way home Joshua leaned his cheek out the window and the wind was blowing his hair. He had a smile on his face and it was one of those times where I wanted to say, "Penny for your thoughts," but since he was oblivious to me watching him, I didn't want to lose that moment. Just as we were pulling into our driveway, Joshua sweetly said, "Thank you for driving on my fieldtrip. Today was the first day I have ever felt special." Bernie Siegel said, "Life is an opportunity to contribute love in your own way."

"What does love look like?
It has the hands to help others.
It has the feet to hasten to the poor and needy. It has eyes to see misery and want.
It has the ears to hear the sighs and sorrows of men.
That is what love looks like."
St. Augustine, Theologian

QUINN

Quinn was a bubbly, resourceful 7-year-old second grade girl who didn't miss a beat. She had shoulder length brown hair and big brown eyes and loved to play with dolls. When both her parents went to jail after a drug bust, she and her siblings went into foster homes. Even so, she had an amazing attitude. She had only been here a month when we found ourselves planning her 7th birthday. Quinn couldn't believe that the whole family was really going to celebrate her birthday, have a special dinner of her choice, a cake with candles, and presents. From experience, we knew that this might be the only special birthday celebration Quinn would ever have. She said she had always wanted a "princess" birthday, so we chose that as the theme, complete with a castle cake, and many specially wrapped gifts - one from every family member - even the babies! Quinn got some cozy pink slippers, a thick pink princess bathrobe, two 'Bratz' dolls, some light pink nail polish with sparkles, lip gloss, some new clothes and special lotion. She got to choose what we were having for dinner. She chose "rice." After dinner (which included some other foods in addition to the rice, of course-) the candles were lit, and the cake was placed on the table in front of her as we all started singing the 'Happy Birthday' song. She just couldn't believe her birthday cake had a castle and sparkles on it, and pink writing that read, "Happy Birthday, Quinn!" She was so excited. She was squealing and said, "I can't believe this - My dream came *true!* I just *can't* believe this - *My dream came true!!!*" The candles were practically melted down to the cake when she finally made a wish and blew them out. Smiling, her foster brother commented, "Jeepers, Quinn! Haven't you ever gotten a cake before?" "Well," she answered, "Not really, but last year I got a cookie with a match in it!" For months, she talked and talked about her birthday celebration and remembered every detail. What an amazing joy. It made me think of a quote from Henry David Thoreau, "Our truest life is when we are in our dreams awake."

"The King will reply, 'I tell you the truth,
whatever you did for one of the least of these
brothers of mine, you did for me.'"
Matthew 25:40

JAMAR

This time, when I picked up two-day-old drug-exposed Jamar from the hospital, the birth mother was long gone. After getting home, I gave him a nice massage and put him in a soft, clean gown. Jamar enjoyed being rocked in my arms, and after a warm bottle fell fast asleep. This was a good time to call and introduce myself to the baby's birth mom, and let her know that I would take great care of her beautiful little baby boy. My hope was that this reassurance would help her to avoid worrying about him, and allow her to be able to focus solely on staying clean and working her drug treatment program. I assumed she was African American, well, because her baby was, but didn't really think anything of our differing ethnicities until at one point while we were talking, she threw the phone down and yelled to her mother to pick up the other line. I heard her screaming in the background, *"I don't want no white girl takin' care of my baby!!"* I was sad, but not offended. Dear God, thank you for the opportunity to care for this sweet little baby, Jamar. Please bless him as he begins to experience withdrawals from the methamphetamines. Please bless his birth mom as well. Give her the courage and strength she will need to get off drugs. Break the addiction, Lord, and replace it with your peace. I pray that one day she might understand what "brotherly love" is all about. Let her know that her baby is cared for, safe, and loved. In Jesus' name I pray, Amen. Several weeks later, after Jamar's grandmother was approved to take him, I had an opportunity to meet his birth mom in person. It was clear that God answered the prayers. She looked at me with tears in her eyes, briefly apologized, and while giving me a hug, thanked me for taking good care of him. Thank you, God.

> "Let us not become weary in doing good,
> for at the proper time
> we will reap a harvest if we do not give up."
> **Galatians 6:9**

FRANCIS

Francis was a pretty, first grade girl who was tall for her age, had shoulder length black hair, and made everyone in our house nervous with her unusual repetitive behaviors. After reporting to the school nurse that her "private parts hurt," Francis was subsequently taken to the hospital, and a thorough examination showed she had indeed suffered from sexual abuse. She was removed from her home and put into foster care. Francis was the only child of a single mom who was accused of molesting her. Within a few weeks after getting to know her mom, a hospital administrator, I couldn't help but grow fond of her. It was unusual for a birth mom to be cooperative in scheduling visits and consistently showing up for them on time. She was appropriate, would bring Francis things and even ask if she needed anything from their house. She had a long-standing job, owned a decent car and was more concerned about the child's immediate welfare, than just getting her back. She began doing everything she was court ordered to do immediately, instead of waiting until the eleventh hour. At visits, Francis always seemed happy to see her mom. At home, we all noticed some very unusual behaviors for a 7-year-old. On the first day, she wanted to play "pretend," and insisted *I* be the child and *she* be the social worker. Over and over and over she would ask questions, mostly whether anyone touched me in my private parts. I was ready to direct her to another activity after about 15 minutes but she insisted we play longer. I finally refused to play after almost an hour. At that point, with a smile on her face she said, "I hate you." then pulled some lipstick out of her purse and headed for the bathroom. She climbed up on the counter and applied the lipstick, circling slowly around and around her lips for at least ten minutes. After I asked her to stop and come down for a snack, she again said with a smile, "I hate you." then came to the kitchen and ate some cut up oranges, crackers and cheese. Getting some laundry from upstairs, I lost sight of her. Frantically, I looked around the entire house and she was nowhere to be found. I stepped out in the garage and saw her in the driver's seat of my van! She didn't even notice me because she was so focused on herself in the rear view mirror. Francis sat there, applying the red lipstick like before, over and over, slowly rounding the corners of her mouth and not noticing she was going way outside the "lines." This was a child who we later found out had been molested on a regular basis by her babysitter. Although the mom was vindicated and the child was reunified with her, there was no way to take back what happened. In a child this young, the molestation caused mental problems and acting out that needed intense treatment for a lengthy period of time. Dear God, thank you for Francis. Thank you for loving and caring for her like no one else can. Please bless her, and heal her pain and brokenness. Fill her life with people who will watch over her, and keep her safe. Lord, give her strength and courage to trust in You. Amen.

"The only way around is through."
Robert Frost

SETH & JEREMY

These two really cute boys, Seth and Jeremy, ages 10 and 11, came into the system after they witnessed the murder of their father. As much as I didn't want to hear the gruesome details, and wished they would instead share them with their therapist, they wanted to talk about what happened. So during the initial 24 hours, I got an earful. Normally, in the first few days, I would be trying to help them settle in, get their clothing and needed items, listen and get to know them, figure out which foods they like, explain the expectations I have of them and go over the house rules, all the while keeping stress at a minimum. Explaining the house rules is tricky because on one hand, it is definitely smart to go over them right away, before they have time to break any or get any bad habits started. On the other hand, it is important they not be overwhelmed. The sad fact is, though, they already *are* overwhelmed! With Seth and Jeremy, to keep it light (or so I thought-) I started by having them *guess* what they thought the rules were. It proved to be interesting. "No picking my buggers and wiping them on the wall?" Jeremy said. Hmmm. With a smile, I said, "Right!" "No carving names in the bed with a pencil?" Seth guessed. "Oh my gosh, No!" I said with another smile, hiding how terrified the thought of that was. "We are not allowed to unbuckle in the car when you are driving?" Jeremy added. "Wow! Aren't you smart!" I said. "No getting into your stuff?" Seth said. They guessed quite a few rules, and there *are* lots of them, but they all stem from love, courtesy, safety, respect and kindness. They call us to a higher standard, and in them, there is common sense and respect for other people and their property. Many children today have few expectations placed upon them and in turn, grow up being irresponsible, self-centered and out-of-control. They often have attitudes of entitlement, and are disrespectful. They aren't as happy as children who learn responsibility and are required to follow rules. When you expect a lot from a child and give them consistency, support, structure, rewards and consequences, they feel empowered to purposefully choose good behaviors and reap the rewards that go along with those choices. Here is some wisdom:

Abigail Van Buren (Dear Abby) said, "If you want children to keep their feet on the ground, put some responsibility on their shoulders."

"Train up a child in the way he should go,
And when he is old he will not depart from it."
Proverbs 22:6 (NKJV)

MIA

Mia, an 11-year-old very chubby Hispanic girl, with beautiful skin and big round eyes, was with us for over a year, waiting patiently for her birth parents to complete anger management, domestic violence and parenting classes, and go to counseling so they could be reunified. Finally it happened. Mia was told she would be leaving on Sunday and when asked what time she would like her mom to pick her up, she replied, "9PM!" Being a little surprised because most kids would say, "6AM!" then laugh, because they are so excited to go back, Mia was serious. So, 9PM it was. Sunday came and just after 9PM, we heard a knock at the door. By that time, we had not only packed up all of her things and placed them by the door, but were well past our picture taking, sharing favorite memories, special dinner and goodbye celebration for her. The next day was Mia's first day of middle school and we had even gotten her a new outfit to wear and straightened her hair! She was all ready! The family all supported Mia and with tear-filled eyes, we carried her things out to the car. Her birth mom stayed in her car, buckled in, reading a book. It had taken 27 minutes to get Mia outside, and another 20 minutes to get her into her mom's car. Just after she buckled in, she shouted, *"Oh my gosh! - I think I forgot something!"* and before anyone could blink, she had unbuckled, and gone running full speed back into the house. Her birth mom rolled her eyes. It wasn't ideal that this happened, but with Mia out of earshot, I used the time to talk to her mom and request that since tomorrow was not only the first day of middle school, but the first day at a *new* school, could she please make it a point to tell Mia before school starts in the morning that she looks beautiful, and if it wasn't too much trouble, to also tell her to "make it a great day." With a smile, I told Mia's mom that that was the send off she was used to hearing each morning before school, and I knew it would mean a lot to her if she heard it that next morning. Mia's birth mom rolled her eyes again, and said in broken English, "I just tell her, *'Hurry! Get out of car! You going be late!'"* My heart almost broke. This is the very thing that makes it hard when a child leaves. When you know they don't have a chance of getting what you've drilled into them that they deserve. How hard is it to tell your child that they look beautiful and to (Take responsibility and-) "make it a great day!" Even the little things, like giving a child a happy send-off to school in the morning, have been a joy. Sadly, Mia did not hear those words I hoped she would have heard her first day of school, but even worse, less than three weeks later, she returned to foster care when her parents began abusing her again. Mia was able to return to us, and is amazingly happy and stable. A friend once shared a wonderful saying regarding love, *"Doing* doesn't count unless *love motivates* it; *Love* doesn't count unless *doing demonstrates* it."

> "The Lord is close to the brokenhearted
> and saves those who are crushed in spirit."
> **Psalm 34:18**

LOGAN

Logan was a blonde haired 11-year-old boy, who had slipped through the cracks for a very long time before social services was made aware of what was going on in his home. The living conditions were deplorable; there was little food, and the home was basically a crack house, where at any given time of the day or night, there would be drugs being sold and used. When Logan came into our home, he was not used to doing anything besides surviving. It nearly devastated him to have us listen to him, say that we cared, and want to meet his needs. Of all the children who came here, he had the most difficult time receiving, and his almost constant, sincere expression of gratitude was really touching and provoked thoughts about the topic of appreciation in general. As foster parents, our thanks and rewards are basically from God. They show up as the joy felt when the life of a child is being turned around, and the knowingness that what you give to the child *does* make a difference. In the county of San Diego, our annual Foster Family Appreciation Dinner costs us $25 per person to attend (unless you are receiving an award), which sadly speaks for itself. I know no other volunteer position that is so underappreciated. You might think a birth parent would treat the very person caring for their children with respect, and maybe even show some gratitude. Or a social worker who knows that you are caring for these kids 24/7 as a volunteer, and don't get a county paycheck or benefits or a 401k, *might* give you an occasional, "Good job!" And, surprisingly enough, even a small percentage of the adoptive parents who *knew* you nurtured and cared for their long awaited baby for it's first 5 or 9 or 13 months of life or their child for several months or years prior to their adoption would consider giving you a card or a noteworthy verbal thank you, but for the most part, they don't either. Giving without thanks has a special attribute of its' own. Leo Buscaglia said, "Only when we give joyfully, without hesitation or thought of gain, can we truly know what love means." Foster parents know what love means. It's not just providing a bed to sleep in, giving them three squares a day and running them back and forth to school. It's a drug exposed newborn that is handed to you that you are lovingly getting up with in the middle of the night to change, feed and comfort as they go through withdrawals. It is the life lessons you are teaching, the normalcy you are providing, the memories you are making, and the emotional mess in the child's life you are cleaning up. It is the phone calls you supervise, visits you provide, fears you quell, tutors you arrange, and therapy visits you transport to and from. It is the support and encouragement you give to the child, as you witness them go through their personal healing journey. It is the manners you teach, self-confidence you build, homework you help with, and birthday celebrations you provide. It is the God you introduce, skills you expand, bad habits you help to break, giftedness you explore, goals you encourage and dreams you help cultivate. It is your consistency in disciplining, predictability from one day to the next, planning that allows the child to be able to look forward to things, and hugs when they are needed. It is the guidance and encouragement to *do the right thing*, believing in them and holding them to a higher standard, and not tolerating their bad behaviors. It is your very presence and selfless giving that you are providing. It is acknowledging the grade on their homework, laughing with them and being silly, and celebrating their uniqueness. It is feeding them healthy foods, answering their questions, teaching them forgiveness through our actions, and celebrating their accomplishments. It is like Nelson Henderson said so beautifully as he described the true meaning of life, "to plant trees, under whose shade you do not expect to sit."

"Abuse leaves a heartache that is hard to heal;
love leaves a memory that is hard to steal."
Heidi McLain

BROOKE

Brooke, a 7-year-old girl with long, dirty blonde hair and a very slight build, accused her mother of drug use, specifically marijuana. At the first contact with the birth mom, she mentioned nearing completion of nursing school and that this whole situation devastated her. I knew from talking with the social worker that upon hearing the accusations against her, this mom volunteered to drug test immediately. In our phone conversation, the birth mom shared that Brooke said to a teacher, "My mom smoked some green stuff she took out of a baggie." The mom then expressed shock that her daughter would say such a thing. I tried to encourage her, by commenting that at least a drug test could somewhat vindicate her, whereas if Brooke had accused her of sexual abuse, it would be harder to disprove and much more complicated a case. Moments later, we hung up, and out from behind the couch came Brooke. She had been listening in and said to me with a half smile, "Oh, and my mom did sexual abuse on me, too!" After calling the birth Mom back and explaining what happened, she was devastated and began to cry. We prayed together and gave it to God. In the end, Brooke was evaluated and treated for psychological problems, and eventually returned to her mom. The whole experience taught Brooke's mom to put her faith in God.

> "But those who trust in the Lord
> will find new strength.
> They will soar high on wings like eagles.
> They will run and not grow weary.
> They will walk and not faint."
> **Isaiah 40:31** (NLT)

COLE

9-year-old Cole and his two siblings, ages 4 and 5, were left to fend for themselves, while mom worked the streets as a prostitute and traded sex for drugs. The older two were repeatedly caught stealing fruit off their neighbor's trees. And when the neighbor finally called the police, they learned that the children were not trying to cause mischief, but just needed food. They were hungry. All three kids were very underweight and put in three different foster homes because of severe neglect. When Cole came to live with us, he was in the fourth grade functioning at the first grade level, had nine cavities, needed two root canals, was diagnosed with a Rage Disorder, and was on an adult dose of Adderall for ADHD. He was somewhat shy, had a sweet smile and was very cooperative. The first night I tucked him into bed was unforgettable. Showered and in his jammies, Cole, with his curly blonde hair and big green eyes, climbed into his bed face down and gently dragged his cheeks back and forth over and over across his pillowcase. After several minutes, he settled in and relaxed, looking up at the many glow-in-the-dark stars on his ceiling. Sitting near his bed, we prayed, and then talked for a little while in the dark, before I left his room. Early each evening, just after dinner, Cole would ask if he could go to bed. Not typical for a 9-year-old, I would question him, "Is your body *telling* you it would like to sleep right now?" "Yes," he would say emphatically. "Okay then, let's get you tucked into your nice, cozy bed." Night after night, he would go to bed early. Nearly a week later, I received a phone call from the social worker, wondering how he was doing. "Pretty good," I told her. "It's just seems a little odd for Cole to want to go to bed early every evening, when there are two other boys his age in our home and a whole lot of fun things to do." "Oh," she said, "Well I'm not at all surprised," she continued. "His mom and her boyfriend, and all three kids lived in a one-bedroom apartment and the kids slept on the floor. Heck, Cole never even had a crib when he was a baby!" My eyes welled up with tears. That night, I tried to imagine how any child living in America had never before slept in a bed. My thoughts drifted around and I began to think about life here compared to life in other less fortunate countries. The United States is the only nation in the world founded by believers in Christ who made a covenant with God - dedicating a new nation to God. Born into affluence, freedom and divine blessings, Americans *should* be the most thankful people on earth, shouldn't they? I wondered why more people didn't contemplate why God allowed them to be born here, and not among the poor, and to be blessed with incredible material and spiritual abundance, if not to bless others less fortunate? Martin Luther King understood service when he said, "Life's most persistent and urgent question is, 'What are you doing for others?'" Since a humble heart seems to be the place where the desire to serve others begins, my prayer was that all of America would be blessed with humility, and that more people would sense a higher calling to serve God with all their hearts.

"Do not withhold good from those who deserve it
when it's in your power to help them."
Proverbs 3:27 (NLT)

CARRIE

When a call came in to see if I could take Carrie, the social worker described her as, "a very sweet girl." Just saying the child is, "cute" or "very sweet," or "cooperative" isn't giving enough information about them. A "very sweet" child could have a history of fire setting, and a "cute" child can be suicidal. A "cooperative" child could be a 10-year-old who still wets their bed. That is the reality. No child is perfect by any means; it is just helpful to know any and all challenges that lie ahead in order to be prepared. Carrie was only 6-years-old and the oldest of four children. She and her siblings had already been in foster care once, and her parents had a history of drugs and domestic violence. This "very sweet girl" was small framed and had red hair and long bangs that covered her big hazel eyes. Her shoes were worn, and she had a very broken spirit. A few days after getting her, she started to "spill," meaning she just began talking in a nervous way about her past. It would be best if it were happening in a therapist's office, but it happens in the child's timing, and usually works out that they spill when they first begin to feel safe. That particular day, we were eating lunch when Carrie said, "I wish I could stay here for a really, really, really, *really* long time. I feel safe." Then all the kids and foster kids started sharing experiences where they *hadn't* felt safe. Carrie unintentionally monopolized the conversation, one-upping the other children's experiences. "Oh yeah?" she said, "Well, *my* mommy and daddy left me in a motel room *alone* for a *really* long time with my two brothers and my baby sister!" One of the other kids asked if she was sure her parents weren't hiding in the closet. "Yes." she answered. "I didn't even have to look; I already knew they weren't in there!" Carrie replied emphatically. "How'd you know, if you didn't look?" the other child asked. "Because my daddy and mommy make my two brothers sleep in the closet. They couldn't *all* fit in there, silly!" After the first few days, Carrie said, "This is *so great*! You give us three meals a day *plus* snacks!" She told all of us she was only used to having one meal a day. At bedtime, she never complained, instead snuggled into her nice cozy bed and drifted off to sleep. Carrie was used to sleeping on the carpeting with her dad's jacket for a blanket. When she disobeyed and got a time out, she sat quietly and "did her time." Carrie was used to being yelled at and given "the belt." Remarkably, a child having been subjected to these types of circumstances is often very sweet and bears an amazing attitude.

"We must embrace pain and burn it
as fuel for our journey."
Kenji Miyazawa

BRANDON

One Friday afternoon, I received a call asking if I could take Brandon, an 18-month-old boy who, after being thrown down a flight of stairs, had a broken leg and a full length cast. I prayed about whether to get him, and I got a strong sense in my heart that I should. Brandon was a tiny guy with very straight light brown hair and brown eyes. His skin had a really nice olive tone to it, and was very soft to the touch. He looked scared and let me pick him up, but didn't smile when I smiled at him. It wasn't until after I got home from getting him, that I realized my two eighth-graders had a dance that evening, and not only had I agreed to drive them in the limo, but five of their friends as well. *Uh-oh!* After complaining as much as typical 14-year-old's are supposed to, they finally conceded that the easiest thing to do, was to make the best of it. Because of his car seat, Brandon had to be placed in the cabin of the limo, *with* the older kids. We drove around to each of the kid's houses, and one-by-one, they hopped in, and acknowledged little Brandon, by smiling and saying hi, and expressing heartfelt sympathy for him. Brandon just lit up! He responded to them in a way he hadn't yet to me. At an age where young teens focus primarily on themselves and they nearly always deem little kids annoying, it felt almost supernatural to witness. After the dance, when the kids all piled back in the limo wearing their glow-in-the-dark neck-laces, Brandon was fast asleep. I thanked all the kids for being so kind and understanding, and asked them who it was that touched *their* lives and made a difference to *them*? I was curious to know whether it was some famous person, or just an ordinary person who made them feel special. Every single one of the kids said it was just an ordinary person. Driving home, I realized that the best part about that night was that the circumstances blessed everyone. I learned to trust that God *would* work out all the details when He gives me confirmation to take a child. The young teens had the opportunity to express tenderness and compassion, and see how extremely healing both are, and Brandon received the special love and attention he so desperately needed.

> "And we know that all things work together for good to those who love God, to those who are the called according to *His* purpose."
> **Romans 8:28** (NKJV)

EMILY

Emily was a four-month-old baby with a sweet round face, a tiny button nose and luscious thighs. She did not deserve what happened to her. Her birth mom, while high on methamphetamines one night, fled a motel and attempted to run from the police. Before driving off, she threw little Emily in a dumpster. When I picked Emily up from the hospital, she was noticeably traumatized. When she began to cry, no sound came out. The nurse explained that Emily lost her voice from screaming so long. Apparently, no one rescued her for over *five hours*. After bringing her home and giving her a nice bath and massage, I wrapped her in a warm blanket and rocked her, thanking God that she survived. It took several weeks before Emily started to calm down. Still fearing she would be abandoned, whenever I would even so much as turn away from her for a moment, she would cry, but still no sound came out. Emily was so terrified from her experience that for many, many months she slept with her eyes open. Never before had I seen anything like that. Recently, she had her first birthday. She sat in her high-chair smiling, surrounded by friends and family, presents, balloons, and a little cake with a "1" candle on it, while we all sung to her. At the end of the day, she laid her head down and went to sleep, and yes, her eyes were closed! Emily is a precious gift from God. She is calm, healthy, loveable, safe, and most importantly, loved.

> "When you lie down, you will not be afraid;
> Yes, you will lie down
> and your sleep will be sweet."
> **Proverbs 3:24** (NKJV)

JONATHAN

Jonathan, a chubby, brown-haired 10-year-old boy, came to our home when his dad physically abused him. He had such bad behavior, nearly constantly, that I had to make it a point to watch very closely for *any* sign of a positive behavior to praise or reward. It had been almost two days with bad behavior after bad behavior. This kid was *naughty*! Disobeying, breaking the rules, lying, deceiving, sneaking around, refusing to do what he was told, not listening, and more. Jonathan used the phone without permission, flooded the toilet on purpose, and wouldn't open his bedroom door when asked. By about noon that day, he was driving me nuts, and it *wasn't* a very long drive! Just when I least expected it, he offered to bring the dirty clothes downstairs. I was so excited; I opened a drawer in my kitchen and pulled out my stack of *GET OUT OF JAIL FREE* cards. The idea came to me years ago. I had bought blank business cards and printed onto them across the top the words, "Get Out of Jail Free." Just below that were two lines - one for the child's name, and one for what the child did to earn the card. I got out a pen and wrote Jonathan on the top line. On the second line I wrote, *"Offered to bring down laundry without being asked to."* I explained that the card works to get you out of trouble and make a punishment go away, *except* if you have lied. I told Jonathan that if, for example, he didn't clean his room and I took away the trampoline for a day, he could pull out the card and say, "Would this work to get me back on the trampoline today?" and it would! Jonathan was so excited to earn those silly little cards. He strived to follow all the rules and the victory was his.

"Triumph is just try with a little umph added."
Author Unknown

TYLER

Tyler had long blonde hair, and was very underweight. He had an infected rash on his elbows and right knee, lice, and scabies, all which went uncared for. He came into our home after his parents got arrested and thrown in jail for drug use. Tyler showed all the usual and devastating signs of child neglect. This 6-year-old boy, among many other neglected kids, lived day and night with the fear and insecurity of not knowing what was going to happen next. Kids like this ask things like, "What are we going to do *after that*?" and minutes later, "And *then* what?" Essentially, they have had to act as the parent, and keep track of everything that is going on around them. When they come to our home, in addition to telling them that their job is to be a kid, they are also told one or two things to expect at a time, like, "First we will be going home, then we will be taking your stuff upstairs," to get them used to not having to worry about what will happen next. Giving a head's up is significant in the child's capacity to let go, learn to trust, and in time, know on a deep level that what is said will happen, will happen. For a child like Tyler to be able to relax, predictability is important. It is good for adults as well, because consistently following through helps them be accountable and keep promises when they know that children are counting on them. Often, the foster parent is the foster child's first reference for a grown-up that keeps their word. In our home, after a week or so, when Tyler asked more than a couple times what were going to do next, it was fun to joke with him and say, "Wait a minute! - *What is your job again*?" And Tyler would usually laugh and respond, "To be a kid!" Then he would be reassured that he had nothing to worry about. Even as adults, we can't see around corners, but God can. Thank you, Lord, for the love you not only have for Tyler, but for each and every child. I pray for children to grow up loving You. I pray that they would also have the courage to trust in You, knowing that you will always give them the strength and endurance they will need to overcome challenges throughout their lives.

"Peace I leave with you; my peace I give you.
I do not give to you as the world gives.
Do not let your hearts be troubled
and do not be afraid."
John 14:27

NEVER MIND

by Heidi McLain

I will soon become a foster child. I did nothing to deserve
  this.
Can I stay with you for a while?
Never mind. *You think you are too old.*

I am hungry. I had powdered creamer for dinner.
Could you make me a peanut butter and jelly sandwich?
Never mind. *You're going out to dinner tonight.*

I am sick. My mom didn't take good care of me.
Can you please take me to the doctor?
Never mind. *You have to meet a friend for coffee.*

I have been homeless. I have never slept in a bed before,
  and I am almost ten.
Can I sleep on your son's top bunk?
Never mind. *You want him to have his own room.*

I do poorly in school. My dad was always too drunk to help
  me with homework.
Can you guide me through it?
Never mind. *You have to go shopping.*

I am suffering. My mom's boyfriend broke my arm.
Can you please comfort me?
Never mind. *You will get too attached.*

I am scared. Everyone who ever loved me, hurt me.
Can you hold me?
Never mind. *It's Monday night football.*

I feel worthless. No one ever wanted to be with me.
Can you teach me how to play ball?
Never mind. *You have to take your daughter to piano
lessons.*

I am sad. So many things are bothering me.
Will you listen to me?
Never mind. *Tonight is your PTA meeting.*

I have been neglected. Every night, I wish I were never
born.
Can you help me want to live?
Never mind. *You are getting ready to go on vacation.*

I have lost hope. My dad said he wouldn't beat me if I
weren't so stupid.
Can I come learn from you?
Never mind. *Your think your house is not big enough.*

I have been bullied. All the kids call me "dirty boy."
Can I please bathe at your house?
Never mind. *You are getting ready for a party.*

I have no self-esteem. No matter what I do, it isn't good
enough.
Can you encourage me?
Never mind. *You are watching television.*

I have no role model. My dad left us, and my mom went to jail.
Could you show me what is right and wrong?
Never mind. *You have yard work to do.*

I have no friends. I have never gotten to go anywhere besides school.
Will you take me with you to church?
Never mind. *It would be too much of a hassle.*

I have been abandoned. My mom leaves my baby sister and me alone.
Can you watch over us for a while?
Never mind. *It would hurt you too much when we left.*

I am lost. No one has ever been there for me, and I don't know whom I can trust.
Can you introduce me to God?
Never mind. *You have errands to run.*

I am in need. There are not enough loving foster parents.
Never mind. ***Will you become one?***

INVITATION TO SHARE

Maybe something in this book touched your heart in a particular way. Please let me know about it. I also invite you to write to me about your experience if you were in foster care as a child, whether it was good *or* bad. I am putting together a compilation of stories, and yours is sacred and deserves to be told.

As you know, the system is a broken one and there needs to be change, but without true life stories that bring awareness to what actually takes place, it won't happen. I thank you ahead of time. Dietrich Bonhoeffer said, "The test of the morality of a society is what it does for its children." and our foster children have been ignored.

Unless the investment in children is made,
all of humanity's most fundamental long-term problems will remain fundamental long-term problems."
**President of the 62nd Session,
United Nations General Assembly**

THOUGHTS FROM A PASTOR

Even though I am called upon to speak for God at times, I am afraid He is the only one who is able to adequately answer all of our questions about abuse; however, I will try to offer some truth. One of the problems we have as victims of evil and suffering, is when we hold God responsible because we felt He could have stopped it. Even though God *is* able to miraculously or supernaturally intervene and deliver us, He doesn't always do it. As a matter of fact, His interventions are rare.

The good news is that God *has* promised to redeem us from the evil that is in this world, and that has touched our lives. He has promised to one day bring justice and righteousness into the world, punish those who have committed evil acts, and restore those who have been victimized. He has also promised to cause "all things" to work together for good in our lives. We don't know how He will do this, only that He has promised to. It takes faith to trust that God will fulfill his promises. When we look at all of the evil acts God let come upon His own son, we wonder how a loving God could have allowed it! Yet it was through this allowance of evil that the greatest good has come! God is a *good* God and He purposes to bring good, even from evil circumstances. I hope this is helpful and not woefully inadequate.

-Pastor Scott Gehrman

THOUGHTS FROM A THERAPIST

Many people are angry with God when they have suffered abuse, as though God was a non-protective parent, or maybe He wasn't there at all. God is big enough to take our anger, although our anger and doubt often sadly keep us from turning to Him.

We are all born into a fallen world, a world filled with suffering, trials, and tribulations. Yet Jesus tells us to fear not, because He has overcome the world, and He will never leave us or forsake us. What does this mean? If we read the Bible, we can see that God *is* there. He was there for Apostle Paul, who remained in a sewage-filled prison cell *joyfully* writing the epistles, which have impacted the world for all the generations. Even when God gave his only son on the cross for our sin, Jesus made a promise to the suffering thief, hanging on the cross next to Him, that He would be with him in paradise that night. When we look closely, we can see that God was there all along, somehow easing the way with His grace.

-Jacqueline K. Stewart, MA, MFT

AUTHOR'S
FINAL THOUGHTS

I thank you for reading my book, and hope that you have enjoyed it. My heart just wants to leave a final thought with anyone who went through abuse. I am *so* sorry, and I know that God is, too. You may have wondered where God was. Especially if no one rescued you, you might have pondered or tried to reconcile some or even all of these questions... "If God is so great, then where was He when I was a kid?" or "It was bad enough that I was abused in my home, but then I was abused in my foster home." or "How can I get close to a God who knew all the abuse was going on, but didn't do anything to help me?" or "Does God even love me, or care?"

Believe me, He cares for you. He knew you before you were conceived. (Jeremiah 1:4-5) and He knows every detail of everything that happened to you. He understands suffering. He wept when you were being abused. He hurts when you hurt, even today. Because God cares, He allows people to have free will and make choices for themselves. He will punish those who hurt you. There is an African Proverb that goes like this: "Smooth seas do not make skillful sailors." God will bless you by taking the bad that happened to you, and make it work for good in your life, if you love and trust in Him. You can leave the door to your heart open, and God won't just barge in, you have to invite him. And after that, be curious to see what He is going to do with your life. I dare you to invite Him into your heart, then say, "Speak, God. I am listening." Then don't rely on your own understanding of things, but trust in Him with all your heart. (Proverbs 3:5) Wait on Him and be brave, And He will strengthen your heart; Wait on God! (Psalm 27:14) He wants to take away your pain and fears, and replace them with the peace you have always deserved. May God richly bless your life in ways that no one else can!

"When it is dark enough, you can see the stars."
Charles A Beard

Printed in the United States
205697BV00002B/211-1176/P